# Wordsmithery

*Related titles from Palgrave Macmillan*

Amanda Boulter, *Writing Fiction: Creative and Critical Approaches*

Julia Casterton, *Creative Writing: A Practical Guide*, 3rd edition

Robert Graham *et al.*, *The Road to Somewhere: A Creative Writing Companion*

Robert Graham, *How to Write Fiction (And Think About It)*

Celia Hunt & Fiona Sampson, *Writing: Self and Reflexivity*

John Singleton and Mary Luckhurst (eds), *The Creative Writing Handbook*, 2nd edition

John Singleton, *The Creative Writing Workbook*

# Wordsmithery

## The Writer's Craft and Practice

*Edited by*

JAYNE STEEL

First published 2007 by
PALGRAVE MACMILLAN
Houndmills, Basingstoke, Hampshire RG21 6XS and
175 Fifth Avenue, New York, N.Y. 10010
Companies and representatives throughout the world

PALGRAVE MACMILLAN is the global academic imprint of the Palgrave
Macmillan division of St. Martin's Press, LLC and of Palgrave Macmillan Ltd.
Macmillan® is a registered trademark in the United States, United Kingdom
and other countries. Palgrave is a registered trademark in the European
Union and other countries.

ISBN-13: 978–1–4039–9827–9 hardback
ISBN-10: 1–4039–9827–2 hardback
ISBN-13: 978–1–4039–9828–6 paperback
ISBN-10: 1–4039–9828–0 paperback

This book is printed on paper suitable for recycling and made from fully
managed and sustained forest sources.

A catalogue record for this book is available from the British Library.

A catalog record for this book is available from the Library of Congress.

10   9   8   7   6   5   4   3   2   1
16   15   14   13   12   11   10   09   08   07

Printed and bound in China

*For M.J., RG.J., D.C.L. – and the F.L.Bs*

# Contents

# Foreword

## Patricia Duncker

'What do you have to do to become a famous best-selling writer?' Donna Tartt, the enigmatic author of *The Secret History* and *The Little Friend*, tackled this frequently asked question. She had a one-word answer: 'Read'. I would agree with her. Anyone who writes seriously and well is bound to be an impassioned reader because that is how you learn. From reading you gather all you need to know about form, register, technique, style, metaphor and genre. Most of the university writing courses in Britain are either linked to the Literature courses or include a major component on learning how to read as a writer, that is, reading not only for content, but also for method. Some students come to writing from other disciplines. I know writer-tutors with academic backgrounds in law, science and foreign languages. But they are all great readers in their own language and in the forms in which they write. The writers in this book return again and again to this question, to the different ways of reading as a writer and to the imaginative complexity of the very act of reading. For we can learn from all kinds of writing: classic poetry and fiction, slush, pulp and other forms of narrative media. Of course we all have our comfort reading, which will be predictable and reassuring. But the reading we do as intellectuals is a form of continuing education, a perpetual stretching of the muscles in the mind.

Writing is now widely taught not only in universities and schools, with the aim of teaching ambitious young people how to become professional writers, but also in prisons, clinics and mental heath care, on continuing education courses and for pleasure, as an activity that is part of your summer holidays. Obviously teaching methods, and the desired results, differ dramatically depending on the context. Teaching Creative Writing as a form of mental therapy is a highly specialised field. Some writers in this context are battling to control, contain and express their own experience, order their thoughts, lay claim to their identities and make sense of their realities.

They are not writing with the intention of producing literature. This type of autobiographical writing is a dangerous terrain to cross, unaided and unaccompanied. The attempt can be liberating, a revelation; but many people who have tried to capture and express personal experience have found the process traumatic. The writing which results from these courses is sometimes overwhelming, compelling, on fire with all the urgency and vivid rage of the living witness. But more often it is dull, derivative and self-indulgent. The structures and meanings of the language resist writers who cannot master them. It can be devastating to feel that one's own experience is second-hand, boring and trite – especially if you are writing love poetry. Learning how to escape from, or manipulate, cliché and how to transform the meanings built into the registers of our language is the writer's business. You can never learn these things if you do not read.

Many writers, myself included, begin their writing class by looking in detail at a poem or a piece of prose which sets a standard of excellence for the students. Young people who do not have a long history of reading and thinking about literature need a map of the territory they wish to occupy. Writing is made of language, not merely personal experience, and the language itself has a history. I have never severed the practice of literary analysis, that is, intense, informed critical reading, and the practice of writing. In my experience these skills are complementary and can be taught as such.

The assessment of imaginative writing in higher education remains a vexed and disputed subject. Most university assessment criteria once included dubious phrases such as 'indisputably original' or 'of publishable quality'. I have never found two writers who agreed on a precise definition of 'originality' and how it could be assessed. So much badly written nonsense and best-selling vacuous cliché is published every year that being 'publishable' cannot be a fail-safe guide to quality. The assessment emphasis now falls on more obviously technical aspects of writing, control over language and form, a clearly developed individual style and an intelligent inventiveness. I don't usually assess content as an examiner, but I am beginning to think that it is very relevant when a student is treading an exceedingly overwritten path where many have gone before. If they are not aware that they are writing on themes that are very well worn indeed this is a dreadful indictment of their reading, or lack of reading. Ignorance of the forms and themes that constitute our traditions of writing will effect their language and risk making their work desperately boring. I happen to think that it is a crime to bore the reader – any reader.

Nearly all university writing courses are taught in workshops and tutorials. I use part of the group teaching time to discuss common points and problems; usually issues of plot, structure, grammar and narrative perspective. How do you construct a double narrative and ensure that the reader remains equally interested in both stories? How do you change the point of view without an alarming lurch that derails the reader? Is it wise to write an 80,000-word novel about bullying and murder in the present tense? How 'knowing' should your child narrator be? How can you build a credible fantasy world in which the reader can be confident about the rules that govern the fiction? How do you avoid spelling out the rules in long boring passages?

Many of the answers to these questions are to be found in this book, which can be read like a workshop on the page, a critical session full of encouragement, analysis and advice. And all writers need to remember their readers – to think of themselves as readers. What are you asking the reader to do? What are you withholding from them?

If someone is well read and knows another or several other languages, it always shows in their writing. It also shows in the workshop. If the group does not have a common analytical vocabulary and if the students are not sharply articulate about their critical positions then the workshop will not function well, to the benefit of all. In my experience the workshop members must be committed to writing as a craft and a mystery in the double sense (that is as both a profession and a peculiar miracle), to ideas, to a passionate intellectual life and to each other. Anyone who suggests that they will end up writing in the same style has clearly never taught a workshop.

The publishing industry now has its tentacles firmly clamped around the potential future stars at writing schools throughout the country. Every course has regular contacts with agents and editors. This is a very positive development in that all young writers acquire a realistic assessment of their publishing options. But as a university teacher I prefer to keep the industry out of the classroom until my students have sufficient confidence in their own abilities to defend their ambitions for their writing with verve and panache, and have read enough to know the difference between pearls and swine.

**Patricia Duncker** is Professor of Creative Writing at the University of East Anglia where she teaches writing alongside Michèle Roberts, Andrew Cowan, Denise Riley, George Szirtes and Val Taylor. Her most recent books are *The Deadly Space Between* (2002), *Writing on the Wall: Selected Essays* (2002) and *Seven Tales of Sex and Death* (2003). Her latest novel is *Miss Webster and Cherif* (2006).

# Preface

Jayne Steel

This course book provides a unique collection of essays, all of which explore, in various and stimulating ways, the art and the practice of creative writing. These essays are from an international list of contributors who are professional writers and teachers of Creative Writing within higher education. The book is divided into two sections: 'Mastering Technique' and 'Mastering Themes'. Each chapter supplies an in-depth discussion about a specific area of creative writing and, importantly, stresses the importance of 'creative writing as process'.

# Acknowledgements

I would like to thank Kate Wallis at Palgrave for her enthusiasm for this project. So too Sonya Barker for her support and advice. I would also like to thank the contributors; all of whom have eagerly engaged with the spirit of this course book and worked so hard to supply chapters that will inspire the student-writer. Finally, I would like to thank Felicity Noble from Palgrave for her support, and Geetha Naren and her editing team for all their hard work during the final stages leading to publication. The poetry quotes in Chapter 6 of this book are excerpts from 'Winter Stars' from *Winter Stars*, by Larry Levis, © 1985, reprinted by permission of the University of Pittsburgh press; 'Dragonflies, Mating', 27 lines in total, from *Sun Under Wood* by Robert Hass, © 1996, reprinted by permission of Harpercollins Publishers, The Ecco Press; 'Detail' from *Still Life with Waterfall* by Eamon Grennan, © 2002, by kind permission of the author and The Gallery Press, Loughcrew, Oldcastle, County Meath, Ireland.

Every effort has been made to trace the copyright holders but if any have been inadvertently overlooked the publishers will be pleased to make the necessary arrangement at the first opportunity.

# Notes on Contributors

**Linda Anderson** is an award-winning novelist and short-story writer. Her fiction has been published in Britain, Ireland, Australia and the United States. She has taught at Goldsmiths' College and Lancaster University, where she was Head of Creative Writing (1995–2002). She is Reader in Creative Writing at the Open University.

**Theodore Deppe** is the author of three books of poetry: *Children of the Air* (1990); *The Wanderer King* (1996) and *Cape Clear: New and Selected Poems* (2002). In the United States, his work has been recognised by a Pushcart Prize and two fellowships from the National Endowment for the Arts. He has taught in the Lancaster distance-learning M.A. Programme; in the M.A. Programme at the Poets' House in Ireland; and in the Stonecoast M.F.A. in Writing Programme in the United States. He is writer-in-residence at Phillips Academy in Andover, Massachusetts.

**George Green** teaches Creative Writing at Lancaster University. His short stories have featured in literary festivals. He is the author of *Hound* and *Hawk*, two novels published by Transworld. His current research focuses upon autobiography and Life Writing.

**Graeme Harper** (aka Brooke Biaz) is the Head of School for Creative Arts, Film and Media at the University of Portsmouth. His latest work of fiction is *Small Maps of the World* (2005). He is pleased to have been awarded the National Book Council Award for New Fiction and the Premier's Award for New Fiction, among other fellowships, grants and awards. He is Editor-in-Chief of *New Writing: The International Journal for the Practice and Theory of Creative Writing* (MLM).

**William Herbert** lectures in Creative Writing and Modern Poetry at Newcastle University. He is the author of *To Circumjack MacDiarmid* (1994), and with Matthew Hollis edited *Strong Words: Modern Poets on Modern Poetry* (2000). He has published six collections of poetry, most recently *The Big Bumper Book of Troy* (2002), shortlisted for the Saltire Prize. His next collection, *Bad Shaman Blues*, will appear in 2006 and is a Poetry Book Society recommendation.

**Lee Martin** is Director of the Master of Fine Arts in Creative Writing Program at The Ohio State University in Columbus, Ohio, USA. An award-winning novelist, short-story writer and memoirist, his latest novel is *The Bright Forever* (2005) – a Book Sense pick and a featured alternate of the Literary Guild, the Doubleday Book Club, and the Book-of-the-Month Club. He is also the author of the novel *Quakertown* (2001); the memoirs, *From Our House* (2000) and *Turning Bones* (2003); and the short-story collection, *The Least You Need to Know* (1996).

**Jenny Newman** is the editor of *The Faber Book of Seductions* (1988); co-editor of *Women Talk Sex: Women's Autobiographical Writing on Sex, Sexuality and Sexual Identity* (1992); *The Writer's Workbook* (2004); and *Contemporary British and Irish Novelists: An Introduction through Interviews* (2004). She is also the author of two novels, *Going In* (1995) and *Life Class* (2000). Her short fiction has appeared in *The London Magazine, Pool, This Is* and on BBC Radio 4. She is a reader at Liverpool John Moore's University.

**Jayne Steel** is an award-winning screenwriter. Her films have been shown at many film festivals including Cannes, Edinburgh and London, and have also been screened both nationally and internationally. Her most recent screenwriting work is a co-written feature film titled *Frozen* (2004). Her academic publications with Four Courts, Ohio State University Press, Cork University Press and Irish Academic Press concern representations of the political conflict within the north of Ireland. She lectures in English and Creative Writing at Lancaster University.

# Introduction

Jayne Steel

## Wordsmithery is . . .?

*Wordsmithery* is a text book for university students who are embarking on an advanced stage in their Creative Writing studies. The book is composed to provide an invaluable resource that is practical, stimulating, non-didactic, challenging and, sometimes, refreshingly witty. An outstanding cohort of professional writers from the United Kingdom, Ireland, and North America, all of whom also teach Creative Writing in higher education, have contributed chapters. All these writers have been dedicated to providing this key text for students wishing to develop their creative work and ignite their creative energy.

For myself, working as a university lecturer in Creative Writing has often meant inventing strategies 'to get students writing' as well as looking for useful textbooks that focus upon 'how to write' at undergraduate level – several of which I have recommended during student workshops and tutorials.[1] But there is often a substantial difference between first-year students and those students who have progressed beyond those levels. This book is specifically aimed at the more experienced, albeit still developing, practitioner of *wordsmithery*.

## How to use this book?

Bearing these points in mind, the book offers a user-friendly guide for those who are still experimenting with form and genre as well as for those who are already committed to a particular form and genre, such as poetry or novel writing. It goes without saying, though, that the journey towards finding (or developing) a creative 'voice' is ongoing – and this journey will often involve experimentation with approach, theme and subject-matter. Such a journey can be daunting. But *Wordsmithery* seeks to make this less so through its scope and

1

content which offers both a practical and, of course, a personal range of approaches.

The book is structured organically to provide students with an educational set of tools. These tools offer not only sound professional advice but also innovative and expressive ways through which to tap into the imagination and develop either ongoing creative projects or an adventure into new ones.

Throughout, writing is discussed in terms of 'process' as the contributors explore fundamental issues that are vital to the craft of writing – and writing well. Exercises and extracts from published and unpublished works that directly relate to the content of each chapter are designed to supply students with direction according to their various needs at various stages in their work. This is why the book can be read chronologically as a 'course' or non-chronologically so as to meet individual creative 'needs' at various points in time. Importantly, the writers who have all so enthusiastically contributed to this project do 'practice what they preach'.

The book is divided into two parts. The first part, 'Mastering Technique', contains Chapters 1–6. These chapters guide students through the more practical and technical skills that are required for particular genres. The second part, 'Mastering Themes', contains Chapters 7–13. These chapters provide a more thematic engagement with specific topics in order to tap into the imagination. As mentioned, each chapter encourages the writer to reflect upon issues raised and put those issues into practice through stimulating and pertinent exercises.

So many students, I have learned, worry that they have nothing to say, that writers are 'born', that writers are a natural breed of the so-called 'geniuses' who represent an 'impossible act to follow'. *Wordsmithery* seeks to give students the confidence to think otherwise.

### Chapter synopses

#### Part I: 'Mastering Technique'

This part of the book begins with a discussion from William Herbert about 'Creative Space' (Chapter 1). Herbert focuses on the issues encountered by those who have experience in writing and some familiarity with aspects of the creative process – but have not necessarily theorised about that practice. Here, basic conceptions (and misconceptions) about writers' habits and attitudes are addressed. These include ideas about the revision process; the inhibitions writers experience when thinking about their own practice; preconceptions about realism in fiction and form in verse; and distinctions between poetry and prose. Herbert's approach is practical and presented in a down-to-earth manner that is aimed at dispelling restricting or self-protecting thinking.

In Graeme Harper's 'Form and Style: Grasping the Tools of Fiction' (Chapter 2), fictional form is considered in several different and productive ways. Harper discusses how many writers often struggle with form, feeling that although they have a story to tell they have no sense of a 'shape' to assist them in the telling of it. His concentration on practical solutions to what are often considered difficult formal questions assists in releasing the writer to experiment with their ideas, trusting that the form 'will come' as the writing develops, and in this way releasing the writer to 'write on' and thus finish their work.

In Chapter 3, 'Hanging Together – Structuring the Longer Piece', George Green focuses upon the longer piece of writing – most typically the Novel. He talks about how, perhaps, the most difficult task of writing a novel is the erecting of the scaffolding upon which to hang the story. Green discusses many crucial issues relating to structure including how to balance character, plot, and dialogue, and the function of the narrator. He draws widely upon a variety of novel styles and genres to examine and explain how there is a basic structure that underpins almost every story, and how this can be learned and used by every writer to give their story pace and drama.

In 'Making Fiction from Fact, Making Fact of Your Fiction' (Chapter 4), Graeme Harper suggests methods for making 'the familiar' into the 'spectacular'. He argues that although new writers often feel they have nothing to write about, the opposite is true. Harper also discusses how much of the art of fiction writing is the creation of the unique from what the writer might well think is the ordinary. His chapter draws upon the work of fiction writers to explore the nature of fiction and its relationship with the 'real' world; and the ways in which fiction plays a key role in bridging the gap between the observed and the imaginable.

Chapter 5, 'Narrative Point of View: Who Tells the Story?', is by Linda Anderson who shows how point-of-view is the most important and empowering aspect of narrative fiction to learn. Anderson discusses the idea that many new writers are simply unaware of the range of possibilities and effects of point-of-view as well as the need to allow space for readers to interpret the story rather than having everything explicitly revealed. She also challenges the way that the topic of point-of-view is often taught in an overly technical and complicated way that can, unfortunately for the student, be accompanied by prescriptive advice including recommendations to avoid certain points-of-view.

In 'The Journey A Poem Makes', Chapter 6, Theodore Deppe takes his reader on the journey which culminates in the birth of a poem. Deppe explains how this journey is a metaphor for the way a poem can unfold and how many good poems end up in quite different places than they began. For Deppe, a poem only finds its true subject after reaching 'milestones along the way'. Along with this idea, the writer must 'pack for the journey'; be wary of the dangers of over-planning; stay open to surprise; become a 'tourist and traveler'; and 'get off the beaten track'. This, we learn, is how true poetic journeys really begin.

### Part II: 'Mastering Themes'

This part of the book begins with 'About A Life: Writing from the Self' (Chapter 7). Here, George Green looks at Life Writing and how this genre is fast increasing in popularity, not least because the material is so readily at hand. He debates the advantages and pitfalls of this genre, and asks what do we – as writers – need to think about before we share our memories with the world? He asks 'what makes an honest book?', then explores the various strands of life-writing, memoir, auto/biography, and witness and survivor literature. Green also investigates the (increasingly blurred) line between fact and fiction.

In Chapter 8, 'People Under Pressure: Making Your Characters Choose', Jenny Newman looks at the ways that writers, from Charlotte Bronte to Ian McEwan, give their characters big and small moments of choice which kick-start plots; heighten tension; sharpen points of view; and keep the reader gripped to the final page. Newman discusses how characters spring to life when forced to decide about something crucial and demonstrates how all great plots are products of these choices. Step-by-step, this chapter guides us through devices that not only launch characters into making choices but sustain the pressure of such choices throughout a narrative to keep the tension building until the conclusion.

Chapter 9 focuses upon 'Writing Food' in imaginative and meaningful ways and argues that, from Keats to Kafka, food makes sensuous, sensory, significant, seductive, surreal, and surprising appearances in creative work. The chapter talks about how writing food, and the related subjects of eating and hunger, supplies the writer with an ideal creative space for deploying the senses (touch, smell, sight, and taste), metaphor and symbolism, characterization, narrative development, and pivotal moments in a plot. There is also consideration of the ways in which food can disgust, excite, intimidate, alienate, and reconcile – and also how food is a pleasure through which to indulge the imagination.

In Chapter 10, 'Children in Fiction', Lee Martin highlights an interpersonal dynamic that lends much tension to fiction, that being the relationships between children and adults. Martin shows how the intersection between children and adults (or families) gives dimension to characterization and narrative. Central issues discussed include the sources of tensions between children and adults; the emotional sophistication of children; the clash between adult siblings, or adult parents and children; the story that relies on the point-of-view of a child; the story that features an adult looking back at childhood; and the story in which an adult's narrative arc is influenced by his or her relationship with children.

'Writing Home', Chapter 11, is by Jenny Newman who explores a series of famous fictional rooms to demonstrate how the use of domestic space can reveal and develop character; generate conflict; bring back-story to life; and deepen and complicate plot. This chapter investigates how characters can be defined by the place they call home, and why they often exchange that place for another. Newman encourages us to think about how an imaginative and innovative 'writing of houses' can function to actually *show* characters and summon tone, genre, atmosphere, and mood. She also discusses houses as being imprisoning or liberating spaces and important locations for 'memory'.

In Chapter 12, 'Bodily States', Linda Anderson discusses how, because people are 'embodied', it is possible to create a powerful sense of the bodily existence of fictional characters in order to make them believable. She explains the ways in which writers can use and adapt their own physical experiences and outlines techniques for inventing characters in terms of their 'bodily lives'. The body as a storehouse of memory is likewise explored, including how scars, blemishes, or stretch marks can inscribe a character's history upon his or her body. Anderson also discusses 'how to write sex' and the use of bodily dramas and transformations as ways of creating points of growth and change for characters.

Chapter 13, 'Writing the Landscape', is by Lee Martin who invites writers to 'Write where you know'. This chapter takes as its impetus the claim that, whether by birthright or adoption, fiction writers use particular landscapes to give their writing authority; contribute to characterization; suggest plots; influence tone and atmosphere; and manage point-of-view. Martin explores the link between setting, character, and incident as well as the notion that if we know a geographical landscape intimately, we also know the culture of the place and its people. The authority a vivid rendering of landscape can add to a piece of fiction, and the way that a writer can use landscape as a conductor and container of emotion, is likewise highlighted.

### Note

1. For example, *The Creative Writing Course Book: Forty Authors Share Advice and Exercises for Fiction and Poetry*, ed. J. Bell (London: Pan, 2001), an excellent many-voiced source of inspiration for aspiring writers. *The Writer's Workbook*, eds. J. Newman, E. Cusick and A. La Tourette (London: Arnold, 2000), a sound practical guide. *Pretext: Salvage*, eds. J. Bell and P. Magrs (Cambridge: University of East Anglia, 1999) and *Pretext: Volume 2*, eds. J. Bell and P. Magrs (London: Pen & Inc., 2000), these texts supply inspirational anthologies of writing from various authors.

# Part I

# Mastering Technique

# 1

# Creative Space

William Herbert

---

**Part One: Entering creative space**

This chapter is about getting into the creative space in your head, and what you might do when you're there. It examines not how we write, but what it feels like. This may help you establish the difference between writing as an obsessive vocation and the amiable doodling that is its amateur counterpart. Any of us may already be or can become a writer. All of us are in constant danger of reverting to the doodler.

There's a song by Pere Ubu called 'Flat' about an incident which took place in Kansas around 1900.[1] Two cars collided. That's all, except the state of Kansas is very flat – and these were the only two cars in it at the time. The imagination can seem like this: an enormous territory, in which any kind of speculation could take place – and a few parts of our psyche bumble around in it like Laurel and Hardy. We call these 'poetry' and 'prose' to cover up the fact we don't really know how they work. What we mean is we don't know our way around Kansas.

### The elusiveness of imaginary objects

Let start by examining something close to hand: what ordinary things look like in the imagination. Think of a domestic object, which you may possess or remember. We have thousands of these pouring through our heads in a river of bric-a-brac: commodities we wish to purchase, heirlooms we'd like to inherit, things that caught our eye in a film or walking down the street. People don't usually try to retain such things − but the writer's object must stay in the brain, even when all the other thoughts distract us into looking at them. We must see it intensely to tell if we're going to use it and, if so, how we can make someone else see it, intensely.

Turn your imaginative focus on the object. Examine its texture, those tears or cracks which say it has been handled. Or is it squeaky clean, like it's been cosseted. Does it make you think of a person? Is it indoors or out? Is it in another country, another century, or another planet? Who was the last person to touch it and what did they do last night? Who will be the next person to walk past it and what will they write down, tonight, in a letter to their sister? Now relax and reflect.

Did your object spring into relief or remain fuzzy? Was it easier to concentrate on the person, or was no-one there? Did it remind you of another object and was that more resonant? Did it make you think of a principle? The answers to these questions tell you what kind of creative individual you are right now.

If you wrote any of that down, congratulations − the biggest war most of us fight is not with lack of inspiration, but with writing things down. Our ego presumes we will remember phrases and ideas, when we rarely have before. Notice it's hard to concentrate on objects in creative space because they exist less in themselves and more in the images or the characters they summon. So this first difficulty, in really seeing the things we imagine − together with my guarantee you will forget most of the interesting stuff − is why we must write things down. Writing things down is the passport to the imagination. Thinking about writing them down is like looking in a brochure and never making the journey.

Words are the unit of currency in Kansas, not our feelings or our deeper spiritual impulses, or any of the things we think make us write. Writers have this fond belief that words can contain their real uncut selves. But this is like expecting a camera to capture not just your likeness, but your soul. You might think a certain confessional piece you've written is really important, and so it might have been, for you. But the only bit that worked as writing was, say, a detailed description of the view from your grandmother's window.

No-one owns language, and when we try to invest words with powerful private meanings, we meet our match in an equal and opposite force: the reader. No-one is less self-critical or more self-indulgent − except for the writer bent on self-expression. The reader identifies with whichever character they like – villain, hero, piece of furniture. They read a collection of poetry backwards, associate freely on one theme and ignore another (rarely the ones you consider vital and obvious). And they stop reading for the flimsiest of excuses. But the reader is not stupid, prejudiced, or obsessed, like many writers – these freedoms are nothing less than his or her rights and privileges. Even more powerful than the reader's veto is the capacity of language to govern itself, whatever our intentions.

### The heaven and hell of drafting

Write down in your left-hand margin your favourite place, then your favourite time of day, then your favourite time of year. Beneath that note your favourite piece of music, and beneath that your favourite book or part of a book. Beneath that write your favourite word. Don't give yourself a lot of time to think about this – the imagination works best when you're off-guard, before your ego gets time to make everything sound 'significant'.

Now go down the opposite margin putting in the opposites: your least favourite place, time of day, time of year, piece of music, book, and word. Don't agonise over the selection because all this information is provisional: you might come up with something else tomorrow. You might fill in a different song, depending on something you're about to hear; you might substitute film for books. But at least you have written something down, and it is therefore an entry point to creative space.

Reading down the left column, we find you in Happy Joyland; reading down the right, Pittsville Direct. These are snapshots of a personal Heaven and Hell, so let's imagine them going on, like Heaven and Hell, forever. Would you still like the only tune on the divine jukebox after a million years? How will you feel about that least favourite book after a hundred thousand reads? It's still the only volume on Hell's shelves.

That's what it's like putting words down on paper: you're stuck with terms that don't even begin to describe you, forever – or at least until you score them out. But the next thing you write provokes the same dilemma: do these words represent me in my entirety, and if not, how can I live with them? The same is true of any character you create, or any scene you describe. So how can writers pass from the ideal – that unwritten masterpiece which is a masterpiece precisely because it remains unwritten – to the half-baked draft? Because we are engaged in a compromise with the limitations of language. The

associations possible from any term are not necessarily the ones that
the writer would like, and part of the writing process must involve
anticipating the reader's wilder imaginative forays. Because that's
exactly what you want the reader to do: imagine things wildly.

Look at your page. This is a little machine, which will take you into
not only creative space, but also create writing. There are thousands
of machines like this called exercises, which expand from specific
phrases or recombine them to create further patterns of language, and
this in a sense is all writing requires from us. The poet W. S. Graham
once asked cautiously, 'What is the language using us for?' Let's
find out.[2]

### More Heaven and Hell

Imagine writing a poem about your favourite place at your favourite
time of day, or setting a fictional character in that real territory.
Imagine writing free-form to that favourite piece of music. Imagine
someone for whom all your most hated categories are a few of their
favourite things, someone who is your polar opposite. Put them in
your favourite book and imagine the scene that would have to be
written: would they get on with the villains? Might they have a closer
relationship with your favourite character than you would?

Link up your machine with five other people's and produce a list
of your favourite and least favourite words. Institute a rule: two characters in a dialogue must each say one term in each exchange; or a
poem must be in two stanzas, one containing the liked and the other
the disliked terms, one per line. I'm emphasising the diverse possibilities here because exercises make clear that the writer's real problem
is not finding a subject, but choosing one out of a proliferation of
possibilities.

If we are to get anything worthwhile out of an exercise, we have
to be better than it. And remember, it's not like maths: as long as you
write something you can work on, you can't get it 'wrong'. This leads
me to a debate that rages in Kansas: work versus inspiration. People
sometimes tell me they're not writing because they're not inspired,
but when I ask them what this means the mists roll in. 'Inspiration is,
er, it's that thing that happens when you're, um, inspired.' Talk to a
novelist about inspiration and a good percentage laugh in your face.
To write a novel you need to sit down every day and crank it out –
if what you crank out is good, then you're lucky; if it's bad, you've
got tomorrow to make it better. Waiting for inspiration disrupts your
ability to re-enter the book's created world.

What about poets, surely they need to be inspired? So why did W.H. Auden go to bed at nine and get up at six, every day of his drink-sodden, drug-taking life, if not to put in those hours with the blank sheet and the scribblings out?[3] The disagreeable fact is that writing is the worst kind of discipline: a self-imposed one. If you're lazy (like me), you try and get away with as little as possible, and you may even justify this posture with declarations like, 'Poetry gets artificial when you revise it: you should preserve the beauty of the moment of inspiration.' No, poetry is one of the most artificial activities going. To assert that you are writing 'poetry' is to sound, to many people, conceited. Of course, everyone ought to be able to reach for a pen whenever they want to, but generally speaking it isn't a mode our society encourages, and a large amount of our psyche is trying to keep us within society and out of the mental homes.

### The Sneerers and the (Un)inspired

As ways round this, writers sometimes fall into a couple of camps – the settlers of Kansas. One is the Sneerers: people so terrified of being ridiculed that they get in first and ridicule everyone else. There's one in most workshops whose criticism is unnecessarily savage and whose own work never shows up, or is surrounded by such preciousness that no-one decent returns the favour. If you slip into this mode, remember: everyone is reading your work through such clouds of resentment that you won't get a helpful response – the very thing a Sneerer needs. What they're really giving voice to is the Inner Censor, whose critique isn't directed at our writing, but at our daring to write at all.

Then there's a group I've already alluded to: the Inspired, or rather the Uninspired; those who wait (and wait) for inspiration. These people find writing exercises so unnatural that they won't do them; suggestions as to how they could redraft are, well, uninspiring. They tend to say, 'That's not the way I write.' They tend to mean, 'I'm going to stick to the few things that usually work.' Although they appear to acknowledge the fecundity of the imagination, they actually emit a giant 'NO', filtering out any difficult material which risk-taking produces. In this sense 'inspiration' is the opposite of creativity. Being creative means accepting that you don't know what might work, so you have to write things down to discover what's good or bad.

We all fall into these modes at some point, and must occasionally get tough with ourselves (as opposed to being sensitive to ourselves).

If you want to enter creative space you have to put your ego as far as possible to one side. If inspiration strikes, it won't by definition be coming from a conscious area, so what does your ego have to do with it? If inspiration doesn't strike, you have to work hard with language. And that means dealing with the limitations that occur when your ideas are bound by the few words of the current draft. Then there are the possible interpretations of the reader, and the possibility that he or she may come up with a reading which not only eluded you, but is better than yours. To do all of these things at the same time as you write, you have to think differently. Keats called this different thinking Negative Capability, and Auden described it as follows:

> What makes it difficult for a poet not to tell lies is that, in poetry, all facts and all beliefs cease to be true or false and become interesting possibilities. The reader does not have to share the views expressed in a poem in order to enjoy it. Knowing this, a poet is constantly tempted to make use of an idea or a belief, not because he believes it to be true, but because he sees it has interesting poetic possibilities.[4]

I don't think this definition should be limited to poetry, since the novelist also builds from world views he or she may not share. And I would place this suspension of judgement in order to explore possibilities at the start of the creative process. It is in effect the moment at which one enters creative space.

### The silliness barrier

When my wife gave birth to our daughter, we were living in a small cottage outside Elgin, and I used to pop Izzie in a sling and stroll around a nearby loch called Millbuies. This was a trout loch, created by flooding a fir-lined valley. It wasn't deep, and there was one point where an old copse, chopped off abruptly, stuck out of the water. For me, this was the object I asked you to imagine earlier: it was difficult to see in the imagination. So I noted it was like the fingers of a hand drawing together. (I captioned the phenomenon with an image, however rudimentary.) As I walked round, I felt that there was a further idea attached to this lopped copse that I couldn't quite see. (Nonetheless, I attached a draft phrase 'lopped copse' to my draft image.)

Weeks later, I was sitting in my study and noticed that I hadn't dusted my window-sill, and that it had some dead flies on it. It came to me that the lopped copse looked like the legs of a dead fly. You know the way a fly lies on its back and its legs draw together? At this point I reached a certain barrier in the creative process.

It's called the Silliness Barrier, or a Haha. A Haha prevented livestock straying onto the lawns of stately homes. Viewed from the house it was invisible, but walking out you would come upon a step down into the landscape which kept cattle at bay.

Here I was with an image of a huge drowned fly lying on its back in a small loch with its feet sticking out – original, certainly, but also ridiculous. This is the point at which people can feel uncomfortable. They hear the laughter of the potential reader; the inner critic sharpens his knives. It corresponds to the other sticking points I've described. But the Silliness Barrier is located within the writing process, if only just. Get over it, and you're into Kansas and theoretically can go anywhere you please.

So how do you get over it? Well, as Auden said, 'Look if you like, but you will have to leap . . . .'[5] Eventually a writer acquires, usually by writing enough rubbish, a thick enough skin to withstand their fear both of the reader and of the Inner Censor. You'll know when this professional dispassionateness has been achieved by an absence of concern as to whether one appears silly or not.

How is this possible? Because something becomes clear that would have occurred to us years ago, if we hadn't been obsessed with inspiration: it's only a draft. So what if a draft sounds silly? You don't have to print it. You won't go down in history as the writer who came up with that really silly idea – as long as you persist in your silliness. Leap the Haha and go in search of the moment in which your chain of association becomes sensible again, and you can guarantee you will have produced an original line of thought. If it contains a striking phrase or a strong image, then you have a good draft. You have entered creative space at a fair speed and heading in a direction of your own choosing. Write into the risk rather than away from it and you will find everything looks different, not least where you're going.

## Part Two: Manoeuvring in creative space

Here I must return to Laurel and Hardy crashing cars in Kansas, and rearrange the writing world into two tribes: prose-producing Hardyistas and poetry-writing Laurelites. For reasons I'll explain, please assume that you are both: the greatest cinematic pairing in one bulgy head.

### The why? chain

Earlier I asked you questions about how distinctly you could see in creative space. I was subjecting you to a technique my daughter used all the time when she was younger: 'Dada, is Great-Granny's ghost watching me when I do a poo?' Asking questions gave her a grounding in reality: asking questions then making up the answers can give you a grounding in realism.

The question doesn't have to be 'Why?' It could be 'Where?' 'When?' 'How?' – anything that illuminates the cranial darkness. Ask yourself, 'What is the fictional carpet in this made-up hall like?' You'll give your characters somewhere to walk. Ask, 'Are there makie-up pictures on the imaginary wall? What are the invented people in them doing?' You will give your characters something to look at and, possibly, a past. The story behind one of those pictures may be more interesting than the present story, and so you may have to start again.

As far as the imagination is concerned, there are only the limits of the world you have so far created, which can be expanded in any direction at any time. The Why? Chain combines the business of invention with the process of revision. Without invention your writing lacks depth, without revision it lacks flexibility and focus.

Compare this to a dream. In a dream, whilst you sit in a bus driven by a purple-caped ape with an Elizabethan gentleman sitting next to you made of chalk, and you don't know why but you're terrified of him, the bus conductress doesn't say, 'I'm sorry, this dream has run out of inspiration. If you stay in your seat some sexually-dubious imagery will come along later which you will unquestioningly accept as reality.' Our imagination appears to be as inexhaustible as our faith in it. It cannot endure a vacuum, and if you ask it the right questions it will fill up with useful junk.

And of course what you've already invented keeps having to be changed to accommodate what you are currently discovering. Para-doxically, this can be creatively liberating. Try the following exercise with your writing group.

### The exquisite arm-wrestler

On a sheet of paper write down a place you've a slight acquaintance with. Describe it in a single phrase. Fold the paper down to conceal this and pass it to the person on your left. Now, on the sheet you have received, write down a time of day and describe the weather. Fold and pass. Now a gender. Fold and pass. Now an age. Fold and pass. Now appearance: stocky, green hair, favourite dress. Fold and pass. Finally a profession or obsession. Fold and pass.

Look at all the information on the page you've received. Roughly, it will fall into two categories. In one, everything appears coherent, as though written by a single mind. The other category will be the 2-year-old six-foot tall female arm-wrestler in the middle of a boating pond at 3a.m. Reach for your Why? Chain. Your first question here applies generally to revision: how little do I have to revise to make this believable? This is the creative equivalent of Occam's Razor: little changes can have sufficient consequences.

So we have a tall female – this might form a character trait. Can she have the mind of a 2-year-old? Possibly. Or she has a 2-year-old child. In the boat with her at three in the morning? Or it's a suicide attempt, something to do with the child. But boating ponds are shallow and she's six foot: won't her head stick out of the water? Forgot about the arm-wrestling. She's arm-wrestling with her 2-year-old son and falls out of the boat? No. Maybe her son was arm-wrestling and his male aggression depressed her. But it would hardly drive her to suicide. Maybe it brought back an adolescent episode in which she arm-wrestled. Could she have humiliated someone who subsequently killed themselves? No. But maybe there was another reason for that suicide and she felt irrationally guilty but had suppressed it until now. Is she looking at the site of that suicide from the bank? Why now?

By following the chain, revising where need be and exploring variations, it is possible to turn the most unlikely combination into a plausible storyline. The most unlikely is often the best because the pressure it brings to bear on your imagination helps you produce the most interesting result.

So we've pursued a notion over the Silliness Barrier and we've clung to the Why? Chain and slashed about us with Occam's Razor: now what? First, note we're at a pleasurable point: the crossroads between a truth and a fiction, and between us and our reader. Wordsworth said, 'The Poet writes under one restriction only . . . that of the necessity of giving immediate pleasure to a human being possessed of that information which may be expected of him.'[6] This stricture applies just as much to prose. So to whom are you attempting to give pleasure?

Some people find ways of writing which they enjoy, but which prove difficult for their reader to access. Sometimes they say they are writing for themselves, which seems modest enough. But have they shown it to anyone else? Because if they have they've got an audience, and if they wish to keep that audience they must consider them. Suppose I read this chapter out in the pub, and when people politely protested, I said, 'I'm only doing this for myself'? Check you're not lying to yourself about any of your motives for writing, because if you are, it's time to revise. Revision is the point at which you stop talking to yourself and start relating to your audience. Until you revise, you are just hanging around in creative space. Revision is the means by which you manoeuvre.

This is the pencil-thin line that a writer must turn into a thoroughfare: you journey into the hitherto unimagined for no other reason than you want to, and you must bring the reader along because you've made them think they want to as well. Sometimes the difficulty here is not how to write, but deciding which thing to write. Sometimes our own desires may not be our best guide. There is an abundance of pieces we could write, but only a few that we want to. And we have to accept that we will not be capable of writing everything that we want to − at least at the moment.

The area of coincidence between these two sets − what we want to write and what we're capable of − is constantly changing, as indeed are their contents. Becoming attuned to what we write well marks a progression in any writer's development. Because it is not until you know what you can and have to write, as opposed to what you could and might as well, that you can decide whether to concentrate on the Laurel or Hardy of creative space: on poetry or prose.

Some people declare themselves to be poets or prose writers at the borders of the imagination, before they've tried both. Many stick with these decisions for years, and never experiment with their rejected discipline. They treat this decision as an apology in advance for all the terrible things they suppose they'll write. Having bowed down before their Inner Censor, they set up shop without wondering whether they might be better suited to the other craft. So here are some helpful distinctions.

### Poetry v. prose

Poetry does not go all the way to the end of the line. Because if you don't fill up the page you focus on smaller units of language − lines − for reasons to do with their sound or their associations. Prose, on the other hand, not only spreads in an ecologically sensible manner, but also tends to contain characters. It is as interested in these makie-up people as we are in ourselves or our worst enemies. So, if you're not that interested in people and their bizarre motivations, then you may not be a fiction writer. If you're not fascinated by the sounds of words and their irrational associations, you may not be a poet.

Can you articulate why you are writing in your chosen form? The best writing can involve the biggest risk, so perhaps you should attempt the discipline which causes you most problems because then you will be most fully engaged, and most surprised when something goes well. Paul Auster, a poet who became a more interesting novelist, said,

> poetry is like taking still photographs, whereas prose is like filming with a movie camera. Film is the medium for both those arts – but the results are totally different. In the same way, words are the medium for both prose and poetry, but they create entirely different experiences, both for the writer and the reader.[7]

In prose, no matter how beautiful the language in terms of tone or imagery, it is usually at the service of a narrative, it is expository and illustrative. In poetry, no matter how memorable the storytelling or the characters, it is the words that are most important, their noise and their nuances. The unit of attention is different: in a piece of prose it is the sentence or the paragraph, whereas in poetry it is the line and the stanza. Further, most sentences or paragraphs are units of sense, whereas a line doesn't have to be – its sentence may start on a previous line and end on a subsequent one. This focus on what might only be an incomplete phrase tells us volumes about the irrational nature of verse.

With prose there is always a sense of transparency: that the words are in some sense there to be seen through; that the act of telling is slightly more relevant than the manner of telling. With poetry there is always a danger that the opacity of the language might overwhelm its sense. Most poets have their own version of Hart Crane's confession:

> I may very possibly be more interested in the so-called illogical impingements of the connotations of words on the consciousness (and their combinations and interplay in metaphor on this basis) than I am in the preservation of their logically rigid significations at the cost of limiting my subject matter and perceptions involved in the poem.[8]

The poet wants everything, as many meanings as possible, to happen at once; the prose writer wants everything to happen in the best possible order. This is not to say there are no poetic prose writers or storytelling poets. Ideally you're the sort of writer who produces a short story when that is most appropriate, and a poem when that feels best, though in actuality most of us stumble between forms like the Titanic between icebergs. (Did the Titanic stumble between icebergs? I may have proven Hart Crane's point.) Never close down an option until you've tried it out. Never refuse to try anything out because it feels silly: you may be back at the Silliness Barrier about to experience Original Thought.

One of the hardest barriers to break through in poetry can make people silly in itself. Form, or the exploration of metre's rhythmic patterns of language, terrifies lots of writers. They make passionate statements about the organic nature of free verse, and then write stuff which scans like bad metre. This is because they're not listening. We all stress our words in a certain way, and these stresses flow in patterns which contain a certain degree of rhythmic leeway. Form just does this on purpose.

Poetry is language in a high state of consciousness, about its own procedures, and about what those procedures can refer to. Metre and its associates – rhyme, alliteration, assonance – all make apparent patterns of noise that affect us emotionally and intellectually. Think of rhyme: two lines end with words which make the same noise as each other. What could be more random than selecting words on the basis of the noise they make? And what could be more useful to someone attempting to escape their ordinary habits of thought? Poetry is full of techniques for thinking differently. That's what revision is for: it's the exploration of those new thoughts that form produces. If you ignore these patterns, and limit yourself to a first draft of the way you talk normally, then you're just chatting to a piece of paper, and wouldn't you rather do that to a real person?

Poetry is built on the faith that these patterns of sound are significant; that the senseless makes sense. A poem is a mode of transport which takes us to the place in which this happens. Consider imagery: Aristotle tells us that

> the greatest thing by far is to be a master of metaphor. It is the one thing that cannot be learnt from others; and it is also a sign of genius, since a good metaphor implies an intuitive perception of the similarity in dissimilars.[9]

What is the function of perceiving similarities in dissimilars? Aren't dissimilar things . . . different from each other? If I say a hairbrush is like a hedgehog, does that mean that you will start looking after your lovely locks with a spiky mammal, or that your brush will hide itself beneath bushes and eat worms? No-one would think so for a moment, which is why I could write an entertaining poem on the subject and it wouldn't be till the last line that you understood it was about balding and confronting my associated fear of death. That's what the artifice of poetry is for: it's the opposite of prose's attempt to suspend your disbelief.

If the reader casts their cold eye over a piece of rhyming metrical verse, complete with apt yet bizarre imagery, they may regard the exercise as a deliberate piece of craftsmanship. They may even appreciate the playful game structure, its obvious artificiality. So they will have no defences against any passionate message you place in such a structure. Call it the cultivation of disbelief: a great number of poetry's freedoms are won by this back-to-front means. Metre allows you to construct compelling rhythms; rhyme drives you to unusual associations; and an integrated pattern of images is like a well-constructed argument underscoring your well-constructed argument.

## The dictatorship of arbitrary form

You can test this by making up a structural rule, then adhering to it. Decide that each line of a poem will only contain four words; or that your first line must contain within it two words beginning with the letter A, then carry on through the alphabet. Or declare that from now on all your poems will be 17 lines long. Now stick to the rule. Initially everything will feel unnatural. Then you'll find a way of working against the rule, so you'll cheat. Then you'll write something that would have worked if it weren't for that pesky rule. So you'll cheat. Then you'll write something that works and would never have come into existence if it wasn't for that arbitrary rule. Now you'll know when to apply the rule and when to try something else. You'll move on to sonnets or syllabics, and maybe suggest someone else tries out your old rule and be bemused by the vehemence of their refusal.

The truth is, there are no rules in poetry, but there are a number of very strong patterns. You can only discover what these are for by trapping yourself within them. As W. S. Graham intimated, a poem is a 'cage without grievance'.[10]

To sum up: poets think words are more important than people, whereas fiction writers think their characters are. All writers tend to regard words as though they were images, as though placing such and such a word in a text will awaken in the reader that specific net of associations it holds for the writer. But these are faults of enthusiasm, of not considering the reader carefully enough, and good writers always temper their enthusiasm with detachment.

Whether you are a poet or a prose writer detachment is vital: you must tolerate the reader's idiocies because they are different from your own, and will therefore toughen up your revisions. You must listen to the harsh inner voice which tells you everything you produce is rubbish because it's usually right, but you must learn to ignore it at least until the first draft is done. You must revise, because until you do you are only writing for yourself. But you must always begin by writing for yourself: only what passionately interests you will ever reach anyone else. The first draft can only be for you, but the final draft should be for anyone and everyone.

## Notes

1. P. Ubu. 'Flat', *Cloudland*. Polygram Records. 1989.
2. W. S. Graham, 'What is the Language Using Us For?', *New Collected Poems*, ed. M. Francis (London: Faber and Faber, 2004), p. 199. Cited hereafter as W. S. Graham with page number.
3. H. Carpenter, *W.H. Auden: A Biography* (London: Houghton Mifflin, 1982), pp. 424–25.
4. W. H. Auden, *The Dyer's Hand and Other Essays* (London: Faber and Faber, 1975), p. 19.
5. W. H. Auden, *Collected Shorter Poems, 1927–1957* (London: Faber and Faber, 2003), p. 200.
6. W. Wordsworth, 'Preface to *Lyrical Ballads*', *Selected Poems*, ed. J. O. Hayden (Harmondsworth: Penguin, 1994), p. 443.
7. P. Auster, *The Red Notebook* (London: Faber and Faber, 2005), p. 133.
8. H. Crane, *O My Land, My Friends: The Selected Letters of Hart Crane*, ed. L. Hammer and B. Weber (New York: Four Walls Eight Windows, 1997), pp. 278–79.
9. Aristotle, *On the Art of Poetry*, trans. I. Bywater (Oxford: OUP, 1959), p. 78.
10. W. S. Graham: p. v.

# 2

# Form and Style: Grasping the Tools of Fiction

Graeme Harper

## Cutlery

What is the Western notion of cutlery all about? And what does it have to do with creative writing?

Plainly, a knife has a function, a fork has a function and a spoon has a function. The function of each piece is defined by its form; for those who have recently tried to eat soup with a fork or cut bread with a spoon this will be most obvious. Now consider chopsticks. Different in form, they reflect both a cultural difference and, to an extent, a functional difference relating to different methods of creating and eating a meal. In China, chopsticks have been used for around two thousand years. Alternatively, while the knife dates back some two million years, the fork first appeared (in Britain at least) in the fourteenth century. The individual fork with knife combination was not widely used until the sixteenth century. Plainly then, form and function have a cultural background, and they also have an historical one. Interesting, but what does all this mean?

Simply, that there's a creative writing lesson to be learnt here. The creative writer who understands form and function is at least half way toward creating a successful piece of writing. The creative writer who doesn't understand these things is a little like the dinner guest who leaves her fork on the table and dives into her plate of linguine with her fingers, perhaps waving her knife wildly in the air shouting: 'I'll get you eventually!' Manically entertaining it might be, but without an understanding of the cultural, historical and, ultimately, practical relationship between form and function the chances of ever fully 'getting it' are slim.

There is a further analogical lesson here too. Cutlery is a collection of tools. So is creative writing form. There are those who might use the wrong tool for the job and still get the job done. The fork-wielding soup eater would be a good example; they might finish the task, eventually, but the process and the product will most likely be inelegant, inefficient and unwieldy. So form and function obviously work together in a symbiotic way, one depends on the other, and is informed by it. These things are also impacted upon by cultural and historical difference.

On the one hand, cultural difference means that the creative writing of one continent, one country, one region, even one household, is distinct from that of another. On the other hand, traditions and practices build up and become cultural paradigms; these promote similarities in approach within a given cultural framework. Form in poetry is most obvious in this respect; it is interesting in Britain, for example, to see the variety of Welsh poetic forms in the light of those of its neighbor, England. Screenwriting is perhaps least obvious in these terms, as a screenplay operates as an international template for the production of a film. Therefore, to a great extent, cultural difference in form is played down in screenwriting. In terms of cultural difference, and its impact, fiction writing lies somewhere between the writing of poetry and screenwriting, keenly displaying evidence of those cultural and personal influences that impact on individuals and groups.

## You

Fiction writers draw their sense of form from the cultural conditions around them and from their personal circumstances. To understand the process of relating function, or the required function of a piece of fiction writing, to the use of form, getting some sense of who exactly you are is a very good starting point. That's why it is often said that fiction writers need time to get hold of the subject matter they are interested in and to think about how it might relate to their own lives, their own sense of the world and, ultimately, to their own personalities. Easier said than done!

Readers generally, and critics more specifically, can often tell the formal choices made by any particular fiction writer. Even though a novelist, for example, might adopt the tonal quality of their book's narrator, or attempt to give the impression of a point of view that is removed from their own, doing so through word choice and sentence construction, for example, there is still cultural and personal influence evident in the final piece of work. This will reveal who the novelist is and the cultural and personal position from which they are writing.

Compare these three short extracts:

1. Miu didn't allow smoking in her office and hated people to smoke in front of her, so after she began the job Sumire decided it was a good chance to quit.[1]
2. The three of us tore uphill through the autumnal tunnel of trees, three harsh breaths panting across the station yard, through the booking hall and onto the platform where Ruby and I collapsed on the seat.[2]
3. Last night I watched a young woman set fire to herself: a slim young woman, dressed in gauzy, flammable robes.[3]

One is a translated piece, which might make it slightly difficult to compare with the others. However, for the sake of investigation, let's trust that the translator carried over the formal qualities of the writing, as well as its sense and substance. Now let's jumble up the authors and think about whether the formal construction of the extracts reveals anything about the writer's cultural and personal position. Could the first extract be written by the well-known Canadian writer Margaret Atwood? Ignore the choice of character names, and look at the flow of the sentence. Could the middle extract be written by the contemporary Japanese fiction writer Haruki Murakami? Again, ignore the character name and simply judge the formal flow of the writing at first reading. Finally, could the last extract be written by the Edinburgh-born novelist and short-story writer Shena Mackay, known for her skilful fictional tragi-comedies?

Here is a primary difference between the understanding of Creative Writing and the critical study of Literature, whether English Literature or any other. At various points in critical history, one literary critic or another might have argued that each extract reflects the notion of an 'implied author', meaning an author who is, in some sense, an idealized version of the real author, a textual construct. So, for example, they would say that while there was a real Henry James there is also a construct that is 'Jamesian', a textual identity that is not necessarily the same as the Henry James, the person, but is constructed by the textual evidence itself. Various critical positions have dealt with this notion of some form of devolution of the real, live, breathing creative writer from the final creative product – mostly believing there is a need to devolve the final piece of writing from the writer's biographical identity in order to get closer to the condition of the text itself. However, the understanding that relates to Creative Writing cannot do that, recognizing that the existence of the writer as living individual is fundamental to the idea of creation and is reflective of the intentions and dispositions, physical environment and behavior patterns, feelings, emotions and reasons, personal and cultural meanings and rules and relations.

In which case the answer is 'No': the first extract cannot be from Margaret Atwood. The position of the comma after 'her', the placing of the 'and' to extend the initial idea, the particular use of 'so', and the combined formal qualities of the piece, that also includes word selection and placement, suggest this must be someone else. Equally, the middle extract cannot be by the contemporary Japanese writer Haruki Murikami. The use of the words 'tore' and 'autumnal', in the manner they are used, suggests this cannot be Murikami. The passive ending of the sentence, which carries with it the writer's intention that this sentence provides a rollicking excursion ending in a dead stop, is not typical of Murikami's formal sense of pacing. Equally, Murikami is a writer who works on what can be thought of as the internal performance of narrative, so that form is defined by displacement of act from intention: things occur in his works, and their surface characteristics often seem out of keeping with the underlying philosophy of character or narrator, in a way that sometimes borders on the surreal. So, no, this cannot be by Murikami.

And the final extract? A difficult one, Mackay is a writer who *does* often focus on stories involving women, and this extract certainly does that. Additionally, she is a writer who does deal in tragedy, and this extract does deal with that – though, Mackay's approach is most often linked to tragic-comedy, a combined form that highlights insights in wry observation. So, it is unlikely that this final piece is by Shena Mackay. Is this because the act itself is described in too much of a matter-of-fact manner to lead to Mackay's trademark comic turn? Perhaps, though, the juxtaposition of the matter-of-fact with the absurd in fiction can result in considerable comic irony. But more so, there is something not particularly 'Mackay-like' in the positioning of the words and in the way in which the sentence is broken in to, divided by a colon. For one thing that colon, linking two ideas, an act and a character, is reflective of a different kind of fiction writer to

Mackay, perhaps a more self-conscious writer than Mackay, a writer using her cutlery in a slightly more formal manner, you could say.

Of course, this kind of analysis needs far greater depth to complete properly. Equally, it relies on a certain degree of belief in the notion that written creative works do, most often, involve human beings interpreting the world through creative practice. But the point is simple: each of these pieces of creative writing is an imprint of personal and cultural conditions, each is an etching on the surface of communication of something that lies below. And just to confirm: the first extract is from Murakami, the second from Mackay and the final one from Atwood.

## Today

Even the most ardent Elvis Presley fan would agree that it is a little disconcerting meeting someone who still believes Elvis is alive. Strong evidence suggests that time, and The King, has moved on. Death comes to all of us, Elvis included. Unfortunately, the same goes for Charles Dickens, Jane Austen, Henry James and Kate Chopin. So it is equally disconcerting to see fiction being written as if time has not moved on, and our formal sense of it hasn't changed.

It is often said that a good writer is most often also an avid reader. True enough, a fiction writer discovers the choices available to her or him by reading widely and taking notice of what other writers are doing, and have done. In that regard, the established fiction 'Classics' are not to be scoffed at lightly: they're works that have stood scrutiny over time, reached readers in some deeper way, and often contributed to how we view the world. However, they are established, in part, because they are from a previous time. The contemporary fiction writer who does not ever enter a bookshop, or otherwise take notice or what is being published, is simply not going to know what a contemporary sense of form means, and therefore is going to be out of step both with the thoughts and feelings of publishers and, most likely, with those of readers.

Think for a moment about the world of the current generation. It would be too simplistic to say that this is a faster moving, more 'connected', world than was that of Dickens or Austen. But this is part of the picture. What is the sense of communication and human exchange that prevails? Consider the impact – however speculatively this consideration might be – of such things as a 100 years of cinema, 60 years of television, 30 years of personal computing.

Wildly speculate on the possible changes in perception that notions such as 'interactivity', 'The Web' and 'searchable menus' might have had on our sense of form. Likewise, how might a century of flight have changed a general perception of the size and shape of the world? What about the Apollo 11 Moon landing in 1969: did that change our sense of perception, size or distance?

Form is historically composed, and therefore relies on a writer engaging with the nature of the world around them. When the x-ray was invented, writers, and others of course, were drawn to consider its implications for the sense of the world around it. That is, if it was now possible to 'enter' the body, without invading it surgically, in what way did that change notions of what was 'inside' and what was 'outside'? How did it change a perception of the human body if that body could be viewed from the outside and the inside simultaneously, and without damaging the shape of either? As the perception of the body was changed, and as all human perception somehow links back to the perception of the self, how then did this change individual and group views of the world? We see some of the effect of the x-ray in both James Joyce's *Ulysses* (1922) and Thomas Mann's *The Magic Mountain* (1924). Historically, the writers of these works reflected the impact of changes in perception on their writing. Form takes something of its attitude from the prevailing conditions and, as readers of fiction are equally alert to prevailing conditions, a connected set of expectations arises.

The following are two extracts, the first from Dickens's *Oliver Twist* (1837–1839) and the second from Jeffrey Eugenides's *Middlesex* (2002). Both give a good sense of historical differences in fiction writing technique:

> 1. It was very possible that he fancied himself there, indeed; for it was plain, from his abstraction, that he saw not the bookstall, nor the street, nor the boys, nor, in short, anything but the book itself: which he was reading straight through: turning over the leaf when he got to the bottom of a page, beginning the top line of the next one, and going on regularly with the greatest interest and eagerness.[4]
> 2. We didn't move right away. We remained parked, as if it were enough just to sit in the car, as if now that we owned it, we could forget about our living room and stay in the driveway every night.[5]

It's a relatively simple matter to see that, while these two writers might not necessarily have set out consciously to highlight, in formal or stylistic ways, the shape and style of the world around them, the form of their writing reflects the attitudes, pace, tone, atmosphere and intentions of their situation. Form, as with style, is a reflection of the writer and of the writer's world. The best fiction writers use this to their advantage.

**Falling up**

A great dancer can give the appearance that they are falling upwards, arm outstretched, chin out, toward the sky. Though impossible, the position of the head and body, and the use of gesture, indicates a thought, and the audience observes a movement extending beyond the boundaries of possibility. This is not, as such, a kind of cheap conjuring act. The great dancer has a sense of movement, pace and human body shape that allows a piece to be presented within the realms of thought and expression, rather than restricted to the realms of ordinary, day-to-day reality. That is not to say these movements are not 'realistic'; rather, it is to say that thought and expression come together in one movement, which appears seamless, and is not bounded by physics.

A great fiction writer also falls upwards. They do this by shaping their prose according to some method of construction that seems both natural and transcending of the day-to-day work of prose. Prose, after all, is the most ordinary of writing forms, the form most often used for a note or an email, a letter to a friend or a job application. Simple, then, and yet having multiple uses. But fiction is not ordinary prose, it is a kind of dance, an attempt to transcend the boundaries of the ordinary, simple, day-to-day fact that it only really is, by and large, a collection of flat letters, arranged into words on a page. Unlike poetry, which often relies on what might be called the 'transcendental' to go beyond its ordinariness, unlike the screenplay which serves as a template for another form of art, and unlike non-fiction which relies on its claim to be a presentation of fact, fiction relies even more so on how it is shaped, its sense of its body and the body's movement.

Style in fiction – which can be considered right down at the microscopic level of word selection, placement and punctuation, and right up to the macroscopic level of chapters, parts and books – relates to this shaping. What's needed, of course, in order to give life to thoughts and ideas and feelings through the relatively mundane physical act of inscribing on a page or screen is some sense of a way of marshalling prose to say, partly through its shape, more than it might ordinarily say.

## Geography: Metaphor 1

One way to marshal prose is to think of it in terms of geography. That is, imagine a short story or a novel as a map of somewhere, and each part of it as places or points on that map. This means that each portion of the short story or novel becomes part of a complete picture, and adds something to it. Geography, as a way of viewing fiction, might seem unusual; but consider that a map is also simply a flat etching on paper of something that is, in reality, three dimensional. That is the same effect required in the creation of fiction.

There are various versions of the geographic notion. Fiction constructed as a journey is one of them. In this case, the writer might think of a novel, for example, as a matter of traveling from one place to another – sometimes literally, but often only in terms of starting from somewhere, visiting places along the way and ending up somewhere. The well-worn suggestion that stories should have a beginning, middle and end fits well with this journey analogy. Of course, it's far from true that every piece of fiction has these things in an obvious fashion; likewise, journeys can be undertaken in a variety of ways, directly, indirectly, with a high degree of control of their direction, or no control at all and so on. So the journey analogy has many possibilities.

A less obvious version of the journey analogy is the idea of fiction as a kind of vehicle. That is, imagine a vehicle that is going to carry forward your thoughts and ideas and feelings. Imagine that vehicle is a piece of fiction. What parts might be needed to make it move forward, to travel onward and to complete the journey? Imagining the vehicle as a train with a set of carriages is an interesting version of this that a novelist might employ: each chapter of the novel being a carriage, and the train's engine being the driving force, or idea, that draws those carriages onward.

Of course, it has to be said that quite often technique in fiction writing is not so much taught as drawn up from the personal, cultural and historical dimensions with which we all engage. A writer may not actively seek to marshal prose in a geographic or journey-related way, but might do so because it feels 'right'. This natural, instinctive act is perfectly valid as a way of grasping the tools of fiction; and trusting it needs to be encouraged.

## Architecture: Metaphor 2

Not everyone is good at traveling, and certainly not everyone is good at reading maps. A map's graphic depiction of the world quite simply doesn't click for some people; the symbols and names seem alien, and the act of transposing the map into the three-dimensional space in front of them doesn't happen. These people get lost.

And yet, while they might spend hours driving around trying to find their way home, they're more than capable of building the house they live in. These are people who might better see fiction as a construction process, rather than a mapping process. In this way of viewing fiction, each micro- and macro-element adds up to a completed construction, a building. This 'House of Fiction' analogy is useful not least because it reminds the writer that each component does help to create the final one, and that therefore anything which does not assist its construction is liable to weigh it down unnecessarily, or to clutter it up. Of course, some readers enjoy the weight or clutter of fiction, so this should not be seen as a universal rule!

## Mathematics: Metaphor 3

Because a portion of those people with artistic interests see mathematics as the Devil's work, it's well worth exploring, even if just to discover if this is true! Some of the skepticism about the mathematical – indeed, about things scientific – has links to the notion that there are two cultures in operation, one involving the sciences and one involving the humanities, to follow C. P. Snow's 1959 analysis. That is, as Snow argued in his book *The Two Cultures and the Scientific Revolution*, the arts and sciences do not communicate, are thus effectively separate cultures, and this is a major hindrance to solving the problems of the world.

Snow's analysis, which received a great deal of attention, even though he noted that it was not particularly new, is perhaps inaccurate in the contemporary world; certainly the emergence of the new media arts, to take just one example, seems to involve both arts and sciences. Nevertheless, there is sometimes skepticism about the relationship between anything scientific and anything artistic. Some of this, undoubtedly, also has a connection to ideas around 'left brain' and 'right brain' functions. The left brain is said to favor the logical, the sequential, the rational, the analytical and the objective, and to look at things in terms of their parts. The right brain is said to favor the random, the intuitive, the holistic, the synthesizing and the subjective, and to look at things as wholes. Creativity is said to be part of right brain function. And people are said to naturally have a preference for either the left brain or right brain.

Combining thoughts on Snow's two cultures, and the idea that mathematics might well be mostly a thing of the left brain, with the notion that creative writing is mostly a thing of the right brain and belongs to the culture of the arts and not of the sciences, adds up to a degree of skepticism about using mathematics as a way of thinking about form in fiction.

However, for some people it works extremely well. For example, because writing a novel usually involves a very long haul, thinking of it in terms of blocks of work to be completed is often helpful. These blocks might be thought of as being of a certain size. In some cases these blocks might be chapters or sub-sections of chapters, and the writer might imagine these also to be of certain size and shape. In other cases, a writer might work with numbers and imagine a short story as consisting of 10 sections, or 4 parts, or 20 bits; or, indeed, a novel as consisting of 50 segments, 10 parts or 5 divisions. For those who find geometry and numbers useful, looking at fiction as essentially composed within a mathematical framework can be liberating; perhaps a little like looking at poetry in terms of syllables and metre.

The fact is, the left and right brain, and the artistic and scientific, are always interacting. Just because a person favors one or the other is no reason they can't be a great fiction writer – in fact, given the vast number of people who write fiction well, it's much truer to say that these preferences are only significant if they are not harnessed to the best advantage.

## Exercises

Creative Writing exercises are sometimes best undertaken in relation to current projects, simply because this is the writing those doing the exercises are most committed to completing. Therefore, the following exercises could either be applied to writing already in progress or to generating some new writing. Either is good!

1. There is no doubt that one of the reasons form and function are related is that it is part of the natural order of things. Whether

religiously inclined, or not, it's difficult to deny that there is an uncanny link between form and function in the animal and plant worlds; similarly it is difficult to deny that form and function are intimately related in the natural physical landscape, weather patterns, even the movements of ocean currents and tides.

To start, then, consider what kind of formal relationships there appears to be in the world around you. Look at the natural world, and then take a look at the human world, the things that we have created. Is there a sense of orchestration about the relationship between form and function? In what ways have humans introduced a sense of form to the things they have made (e.g. buildings, agricultural environments, traffic).

Now consider if any of the observable forms have a use as metaphoric marshaling tools for your fiction writing. Could your story be a certain kind of building, for example? Could your novel be the migratory patterns of a certain kind of bird or the line taken when traveling from your home to the home of a friend? If it is possible, draw the form of your story or novel. That is, roughly sketch it. Does it have a regular or irregular shape?

If setting out on a new piece of fiction writing, try constructing a story that is based on one of the forms you see around you.

2. Choose three contemporary novels and try to determine what formal structures seem to be at work in them. Does there seem to be a sense of patterning? If so, how would you describe it? If you don't seem to be able to find a pattern, what might this suggest (e.g. sometimes a piece of fiction is so naturalistic in mode that any sense of it being orchestrated by the writer is almost invisible)?

What might these novels, and defining structure behind them, have to say in relation to your own fiction writing? Is your work heavily patterned or lightly patterned? Would you argue that your work, or the work of any of the three novelists, has no real pattern at all? Can you detect any cultural, personal or historical background that might reflect on the nature of the formal structures in these works?

Compare these longer works with three short stories? First, how is the formal sense different? Secondly, is there a discernible sense of pattern in the short stories? Thirdly, how do they compare with each other in terms of form?

Do any of the approaches used by either the novelists or the short-story writers seem approaches you might adopt in your own work? Can you determine what formal patterns you are using at the moment, if any? How would you describe them? Can you imagine one piece of your work constructed using a different formal sense? If so, what might it be? If you compared and contrasted three different formal patterns for any pieces of your work, how might each make it different from its associate? What seems to be the driving force behind your decision to favor one formal pattern over another?

3. And, finally, method and madness all at once. There's been a lot said here about 'function', but very little done to decide what that might mean. When considering any pieces of your own work can you define what their function might be? For example, is one story aiming primarily to amuse the reader; that is, it's a comic piece? Is your novel aiming to provide entertainment while also revealing the horror of war, or is it looking to be the vehicle for the results of your personal investigation into the relationship between a daughter and her mother?

For certain fiction writers, who have an idea of the word 'function' as being somewhat utilitarian, even thinking about the *function* of fiction goes against the idea of fiction having value in its own right. But the word function here is being used very broadly, meaning something along the lines of 'Why does it exist?', or 'What's it attempting to do?' or 'What is the writer's intention in creating it?'. One fact of the contemporary world needs recalling: there is more choice of leisure activities for the vast majority of people, certainly in the Western world, than there has ever been. In which case, as reading fiction competes against so many alternative preoccupations, it's worth considering what our personal sense of the function of each piece of fiction might be.

4. As a final exercise, try writing three or four different intro-ductory paragraphs to a story or novel, aiming to give these different introductory paragraphs different functions. In one case, for example, perhaps the function might be to alert the reader to the beauty of summer; in another case, the function might be to begin to set up the nature of conceit, and so on. There are an infinite number of ideas that could inform this exercise.

## Notes

1. H. Murakami, *Sputnik Sweetheart* (London: Harvill, 2001), p. 53.
2. S. Mackay, *The Orchard On Fire* (London: Minerva, 1996), p. 73.
3. M. Atwood, *The Blind Assassin* (London: Virgo, 2001), p. 528.
4. C. Dickens, *Oliver Twist*, first published 1837–1839 (London: Penguin, 1966), p. 114.
5. J. Eugenides, *Middlesex* (London: Bloomsbury, 2002), p. 253.

# 3

# Hanging Together – Structuring the Longer Piece

George Green

---

There isn't a template for structuring a novel – at least, not unless you are writing something like the type of romantic fiction for which your publisher supplies you with a list of possible situations, occupations and characters, beyond which you are forbidden to stray (there's nothing wrong with that, of course, as far as it goes, and you may wish to take satisfaction from such small epiphanies as you can insert within the prearranged story-grid, but there isn't much room for changing things around when the Muse strikes). Even a novel that aims to stay within a very narrow and clearly defined genre will have its own demands, will always keep suggesting to the writer that there are alternatives that might repay investigation. So let's not look for an exact formula or a definitive map for structuring a novel. It isn't that easy.

However, while there may not be a map, there are guidebooks, and they can help. There are a number of approaches to structuring a novel which can help the writer stay pointing more or less at their destination and not heading off on pointless excursions and detours. But not all approaches suit everyone or indeed every novel. The writer should take from the various approaches what they need, what works best for them. They may find that one particular approach suits their novel and so choose to rely heavily upon that, or they may draw upon a number of different ideas. It really doesn't matter how you do it. All that matters is what works for you and your narrative.

## Starting out

Let's consider the process from the beginning.

You have decided that you have an idea strong enough for a novel. You have probably decided on the large bones of your plot and situation. To a greater or lesser extent you know your main characters, you have the beginning clear in your mind and some idea of how it ends, and you already have a clutch of scenes either in mind or drafted, though probably you don't yet know for sure how they all hang together.

(*Warning*: if you haven't already got a fair idea of at least some of these things then it's probably too early to be worrying much about structure.)

The problem now is simple. How do you plan the novel so that you avoid spending too much time on unimportant things, while avoiding firming things up too early and thus running the risk of restricting yourself too much?

*Answer*: By focussing on what matters.

Forget detail for now. Stop worrying about getting everything exactly right. It only has to be perfect on the day you hand it to the publisher. Before that day, your manuscript can be as scrappy and disorganised and haphazard as you like and no-one except you will ever know. If you do already know the details, fine, write them down now by all means. If you don't, forget about them. You have to build the house before you can hang your clothes in the bedroom, it can't be done the other way around. Sort the small things out later. Concentrate on the Big Picture.

*Question*: How do I know what's Big Picture and what isn't?

Try thinking about the answers in these ways.

### *Approach 1　Drama and life both usually have three acts*

You may have heard of the Rule of Three that governs many of our thought processes. It isn't an accident that most jokes involve three people, nor is it a coincidence that most plays have three Acts.[1] There is a reason for this. Putting it simply:

When telling a story – any story – you have to introduce the situation, you have to develop it and then you have to complete it.

Not necessarily, of course, in that order.

It may help to think about this process in the simplest form of story possible; a (very short) joke.

A white horse walks into a pub, sits down at the bar and orders a pint of beer. While the barman is pouring the beer he looks up, smiles and says to the horse, 'You know something strange? We've got a whiskey here named after you.' The horse looks surprised and says: 'What, you've got a whiskey here called Eric?'

Here's what just happened in terms of the process described above.

*Introduction*

A white horse walks into a pub, sits at the bar and orders a beer.
(This gives the listener the essential information they need in order to understand what comes next. If the listener is not made aware that there is a horse, that it is white and it is sitting in a pub, the joke would make no sense.)

*Development*

While the barman pours the beer he smiles and says to the horse 'We've got a whiskey here named after you.'
(The listener – one hopes – is now leaning forward with a puzzled expression, wondering where the story is going.)

*Completion*

The horse looks surprised and says: 'What, you've got a whiskey here called Eric?'
(The story is finished, nothing more needs to be said.)

A number of useful things concerning the structure of your novel can be gleaned from thinking about it in this way.


*Length and when to bring people onstage*

Your story will probably have three Acts too. The exact details will vary, but as a very general rule you will often need to use around 30 per cent of your total length introducing the situation, the characters and so on; another 40 per cent or so developing them, and the remaining 30 per cent bringing things to a conclusion. These are guidelines, not rules, but they give a useful basic structure. For example, it makes sense that all the major characters should be known to the reader by the end of Act 1, about a third of the way through. Later than this their impact is diluted and you risk confusing your reader, who will not be sure if the character is really important or not. Note that this does not mean that the reader has actually to meet them. Many stories leave a major character to appear in the final Act, or even in the final pages. For example, in the story of *Robin Hood*, King Richard only reveals himself at the very end, but note that his presence (or more accurately, his absence) is the motor that drives the events of the entire story. Think also of the character Kurtz in Conrad's *Heart of Darkness*.[2] The point is that the reader needs to be aware of the existence of the character, even if he is only spoken of in whispers and doesn't materialise in the flesh until the novel is nearly over.

*Pace*

If you are wondering why your novel lacks pace and focus, one reason may be because things are in the wrong place. Check that introductory material comes early so that the story can flow uninterrupted. Make sure that everything is in place by the end of the middle Act so that the movement towards the dénouement can happen uninterrupted. Going back to the joke above, the effect if all this has not been done properly is as follows:

> There was this horse sitting in a bar . . . well, he'd just walked in . . . and he says to the man behind the bar . . . could actually be a woman, doesn't matter, and he says . . . the horse, not the barman, or barwoman . . . where was I? . . . 'oh yes,' he says, 'I'd like a whiskey,' no, it was a beer, could be stout, doesn't matter, and the barman says to him . . . hang on, did I say the horse was white? . . .

And so on. If you've ever sat uncomfortably while someone mangles a joke in this way then you will appreciate the importance of organising your structure in order to present the elements of your story in the most effective order.

*Crises*

This three Act structure also rather conveniently allows for three major crises. Again, you don't have to have three, but it's a useful way to think about narrative. Putting it simply:

- The first crisis usually occurs early in the first Act and precipitates the action of the novel.
- The second crisis is located somewhere near the middle and will often be a revelation which significantly affects and alters the action and/or the situation.
- The third crisis will be the final revelation which makes sense of the preceding confusion and questions which you hope you have been sowing in the reader's mind throughout the novel.

It may be useful to think of each crisis asking a question of the story, which will usually be answered in the succeeding part of the story.

Note that these questions are all *active* – we are not asking 'What happens next?' but 'What will our Hero do?'[3] The difference is crucial.

Here are some specific examples which will illustrate this idea.

**Example 1**: Think about Margaret Mitchell's *Gone With The Wind*.[4] This is a useful example because it has two main plot strands that can be treated separately: Scarlett's relationship with her home, which represents family and security, and her relationships with the two men in her life.

Gone With The Wind

| Plot strand | Home | Romantic happiness |
|---|---|---|
| Act 1 | The first Act introduces Scarlett, her privileged life and her beautiful house and land, all of which she loves, and which by the end of the Act she has lost. | Scarlett has romantic ideas about herself and Ashley Wilkes, which at the end of the Act are dashed. In a fit of pique she accepts Rhett Butler's proposal even though she does not love him. |
| | *Question*: How will she regain it? | *Question*: How will she cope with being married to one man but loving another (who is himself married)? |
| Act 2 | The second Act shows her struggle to regain and rebuild her property and social standing. | Scarlett's relationship with Rhett deepens and we come to understand that they do in fact love each other and are ideally suited, but we also know that she does not recognise this. The relationship breaks up. |
| | *Question*: How will she overcome the obstacles that are in her way? | *Question*: Will she realise her love for Rhett before it is too late? |
| Act 3 | The third Act sees her succeed in re-establishing the financial security which is so important to her. | Rhett leaves and we see Scarlett in denial over her feelings for him, persuading herself that she still loves Ashley. When confronted with Ashley's love for Melanie, she finally realises the true nature of her feelings. |
| | *Question*: Will financial security bring her the happiness she thinks it will? | *Question*: Will she get Rhett back again and find happiness? |

**Example 2**: Think about Nick Hornby's *High Fidelity*, which is *Romeo and Juliet* rewritten and the oldest three-Act story in the business, usually summarised as 'Boy Gets Girl/Boy Loses Girl/Boy Gets Girl.'[5]

*High Fidelity*

| Act 1 | Boy Gets Girl, or, or more correctly, at the start of the book he already has her but we are quickly aware that he is in danger of losing her. By the end of the Act, she has left him. |
|---|---|
| | *Question:* Will he be able to manage without her? |
| Act 2 | Boy Has Lost Girl, and has to deal with it, which he does mostly not very well. He struggles to decide between thinking that he no longer loves her and should move on, and that he still has feelings for her and should work to get her back. |
| | *Question:* Will he decide to try and get her back, and will he succeed? |
| Act 3 | Boy Gets Girl. Having acknowledged his feelings for her and resolved to make some changes, they are reunited. |
| | *Question:* Has he learned the lessons that he needs to know in order for the relationship to go on and be happy? |

Both the above tables are of course reductive travesties of the stories, but they illustrate what's going on. You might also think about any James Bond story, all of which closely follow the same general pattern. In Act 1, Bond finds out what the villain is up to and prepares himself to meet and defeat him. He also usually meets his primary romantic involvement. In Act 2, Bond meets the villain and there is a good amount of preliminary fencing and derring-do which establishes the villain's character and abilities as well as reminding us what a man of action Bond is.[6] In Act 3, the villain's plans advance to their crucial point, and Bond makes his move to prevent their success.

Superficially, the Bond plot above doesn't look much like the plot of *High Fidelity*, but the principle is the same.

Introduce, Develop, Conclude. Beginning, Middle, End.

So, one approach you might consider is to break your story down into Acts, it can make deciding what goes where a great deal easier.

### Approach 2   All stories are journeys

Your novel may not have a story, in which case I wish you luck.[7] Assuming, however, that it does have a story, your novel will almost inevitably involve a journey of some sort. It may be a physical journey such as Frodo's trek to Mordor in Tolkein's *The Lord of the Rings*.[8] It may be a journey of personal discovery, such as that experienced by Richard Papen, the narrator of Donna Tartt's *The Secret History*,[9] and by Jack Crabbe, the narrator of Thomas Berger's *Little Big Man*.[10] It can be a social journey, such as that experienced by *Oliver Twist*[11] and *Jane Eyre*.[12] It may be the journey from childhood to adulthood (e.g. Tom in Mark Twain's *The Adventures of Tom Sawyer*).[13] Journeys do, of course, take place in more than one direction, and can be away from the positive as well as towards it. It may be a negative journey, one of emotional, sexual or spiritual degradation such as that experienced by Marlowe, the narrator of Conrad's *Heart of Darkness*,[14] and by Guy in Martin Amis's *London Fields*.[15] It may be a circle, which ultimately returns the character to where they started, having travelled but failed to progress. And so on. It can be combinations of all these examples and others. Remember also that journeys can take place in the head. Life is a journey, through time and experience, therefore it is unsurprising that stories about life are journeys too.

So, think about what journey your characters are undertaking in your story. If there isn't a journey, how is your story to move?[16] The useful thing about journeys from a storyteller's point of view is that they imply progression, change, activity, movement, and perhaps most especially the potential for several varieties of conflict. The useful thing about them from a structuring point of view is that they have a beginning, a middle and an end; which, incidentally, you may like to think of as three Acts.

Everything (yes, everything) that happens in your story should have a relationship with your characters' journey. The scenes (see Approach 3 below) which comprise the story are the staging posts along the way.

So, think of your story as a journey.

### Approach 3    Stories are made up of scenes

A story is a succession of scenes, strung together with connective tissue. A rule of thumb (which is the closest you'll get to a real Rule in this chapter) is that a full-length novel will have around 12 scenes. If your novel is 70,000 words long that's an average of about 6,000 words for each scene. The connective tissue I referred to above is often also made up of mini-scenes, but we won't be talking about that.

If you are familiar with Joseph Campbell's *The Hero's Journey* (which will repay a look no matter what type of novel you're writing) then you'll know that there are 12 stages in the Journey.[17] Twelve is the number of scenes in an archetypal Hero's story, but it needn't be yours. However, it's a useful way of organising and balancing your story. Too many short scenes will make your story seem fragmented.

Too many long scenes, and your story runs the danger of feeling static and slow.

## Example 1: *Alice in Wonderland*[18]

1. Alice follows the White Rabbit
2. Alice changes size
3. Alice falls into the pool
4. Alice runs in the race
5. Alice grows, eats the cake and shrinks
6. Alice meets the Caterpillar
7. Alice arrives at the Duchess's House
8. Alice meets the Cheshire Cat
9. Alice joins the Mad Hatter's Tea Party
10. Alice joins in the game of croquet
11. Alice meets the Gryphon and Mock Turtle
12. Alice grows again and wakes up.

Neat, huh? You might argue that some scenes have been left out to make this into a convenient list of 12, and I would probably agree. *Alice in Wonderland* is an unusual novel deliberately designed with more scenes than most. Even so, there are probably no more than 15 proper scenes.

## Example 2: *The Da Vinci Code*[19]
A more conventional example is Dan Brown's *The Da Vinci Code*. I would suggest that it has 12 main scenes.

1. Prologue in the Louvre, the death of the old man
2. The Louvre, the scene is set
3. Escape from the Louvre
4. In the vault
5. Escape from the vault
6. Arrival at the house
7. Escape from the house
8. Flight to England
9. The scene in the Church
10. The scene in the big house
11. The Final Showdown
12. Epilogue.

You may feel that this list cheats slightly as the Epilogue is brief and lightweight compared to the other scenes, but I would suggest that it is an essential part of the story. My point here is not to suggest that all successful books have 12 scenes and so yours must too, but to describe the way many books work. If you have a better idea, go with it. If not, this works, so why not try it?

So, look at your novel and ask yourself 'what are my scenes?' A scene will often be a set-piece. Scenes are often the bits that you rough-draft out all in one go. Then, when you think, 'Right, that's that, now I need to get my hero to Paris for the next big set-piece', you have come to the end of the scene and now need connective tissue. You've been dwelling on details, going slow, giving the reader lots to think about. Now make the narrative move; get him to Paris quick. Unless there is something significant about the flight, don't tell the reader about it. Begin your chapter with him in his hotel room overlooking the *Champs Elysees* jet-lagged and sleepy. We'll understand what's happened. Move between sections of writing which are big/detailed/long (the scenes) and small/skimming/quick (the connective tissue). It will give your writing pace and variety.

Remember that scenes are mini-stories, and so they should also have Beginnings, Middles and Endings. Consider the great set-piece scene of the ball at the centre of *Pride and Prejudice*.[20] It begins with one set of assumptions about the relationship between Lizzy and Darcy. Through character interplay the situation develops and changes substantially between the beginning and the end. This scene is crucial. Read the first chapter of Ian McEwan's *Enduring Love*.[21] It sets the tone of the whole novel. The information in it could have been told in a paragraph, but the power of the novel would have been much diminished.

Writing in scenes makes it easier for you to use light and shade and changes of pace to vary the telling. The fact that you are writing a part of the story as a scene rather than going past it at speed suggests to the reader that something notable is happening. A storyteller sitting by a campfire uses pauses, changes of speed, different emphasis, alterations in vocal register and so on to give the story colour and to direct the audience. Writers need to do the same things. A primary fault of many writers' first attempts at a longer piece is difficulty with pacing and emphasis. It's hard to say exactly where emphasis should go without talking about specific stories, but as a rule your 12 (or so) scenes will need both you and your reader to spend care and time on them. The rest, the connective tissue, doesn't need anything like the same degree of attention. If something contributes to the story or to character then it needs emphasis. Note the word 'contributes' here. It may be essential for your hero to get from Paris to London in order for the story to make sense, but that doesn't necessarily mean it requires emphasis. Ask yourself 'If this scene was reduced to a single sentence ("John flew from Paris to London"), how much would the story lose?' The sentence may need saying, indeed the story may depend on it, but that doesn't mean you should emphasise it. The opposite may be true, you may actually be trying to draw the reader's attention away. Whatever you do, don't write the whole story at the same speed. The reader needs to know where to focus.

So, write in scenes and keep the story moving, focussing on what is important and not spending unnecessary time on the bits in between.

### Approach 4   The story arc

This approach draws on the three ideas above. The idea is simple. Every story has an arc, which a writer can use to help them structure their work.

Consider the two axes of a graph. The horizontal axis represents the passage of time in the novel. The vertical axis is the action of the novel. Action can be interpreted in a number of ways. It can be action in the Hollywood sense of car chases and rising body count, or it can be action in the sense of tension and/or emotional involvement. So, the line of the story moves from left to right, in an arc, rising up or down as the action increases or diminishes.

As a general rule, the arc will start low on the left at the beginning, and, as time passes, will rise as it progresses towards the right – the end. This rise may be in a series of small peaks, each higher than the next, or it may be a slow steady climb, or a combination of the two. It may start with a high point (in a James Bond film, where the pre-credits sequence is often the best bit – but note that this sequence is often not directly related to the actual story), or it may dip suddenly before the end, or any one of a dozen other things, depending on the story. The point, to put it simply, is that the story gets more exciting or more tense or more involving as it goes along. A thriller such as *The Da Vinci Code* allows us to see this very clearly. It will start with something that grabs our attention, then allows us to relax (note: the relaxation is relative – the pressure is kept on but not as intensely). It will then progress towards the end via a series of crises, each followed by a slight relaxation, each marking a higher point than the last. The important point is that the overall tendency of the graph is upwards – the story becomes increasingly tense, involving, exciting, desperate, higher-stakes, whatever the effect you are aiming for.

This idea may seem obvious, but it needs saying. A story that starts with a bang and then becomes less interesting is no-one's idea of a good read. The point is that a writer can use this idea of ever-increasing pressure as an aid to structuring a novel, and it can help with character development too. First, ask yourself, 'what effect am I trying to have on my reader, what reaction am I trying to provoke?' Having established that you are trying to make your reader excited, frightened, angry, sad or whatever it is, ask yourself 'do the scenes I am writing build on each other in such a way that the reader never feels that they are being let go?' Once you have achieved an effect, don't let the reader escape. Draw your line on your graph (literally or in your mind), checking that, whatever you may be doing on any given page – and it's always good to let the reader relax just before you pull them over a cliff, the shock is all the greater – the overall tendency from scene to scene, chapter to chapter, is up, always up. Move through a series of crises to the Crisis at the end.

If you have the major Crisis in the middle then you need a very good reason – it's like having the punchline in the middle of the joke.

You can use arcs for character development too. Your main characters should follow an arc, in that their development, or knowledge of their situation, or involvement in something, or exposure to danger, or whatever it is you are doing to them will increase as the story progresses. If you let the tension dip, then it should only be to allow the reader to catch their breath before you re-apply the thumbscrews.

### Exercises

1. Draw a graph (freehand will do, it's just to let you see what's happening) of how and where the peaks and troughs in your story take place. You'll need a time axis along the bottom and a tension axis at the side.

Note that I use the word 'tension', not a word like 'action'. Action is optional, tension is not. A book without action can still grip you, but a book without tension cannot. I would rather read about two people sitting looking at each other in silence where the air crackles with tension than read about yet another ho-hum car chase.

Divide the horizontal time axis into sections equal to the number of chapters (I'm assuming the chapters are of approximately equal length). Give each section two different points out of ten for tension, a high one and a low one, and mark the two points on the graph. Draw a line connecting the low points, and a similar line connecting the high points. Now have a long look at the graph and ask yourself some questions.

(a) Are the points of greatest tension where they should be?
(b) Regardless of any individual highs and lows, is the overall trend of both lines upwards?
(c) Are you happy that your book has enough tension to grip the reader, while allowing them off the hook just enough to catch their breath before screwing it up tight again?

2. Imagine that your story is a 12-scene play. Ignore bits of connective tissue, such as the fact that someone may have flown to another city between chapters, stated in a sentence. What would the 12 scenes be? Write them down. (They will probably be quite close to the sections in the graph in Exercise 1) Now ask yourself some questions.

(a) If you don't have 12 important scenes, are you convinced that your story has enough in it to hold your reader's attention? Note that the scenes don't have to be big or noisy or violent, but they must be important to the characters, important to the development of the story.
(b) If you have more than 12 important scenes, is your book too long? Of course, lots of long books have more than 12 big scenes. If yours has, are you convinced that the length of your book is justified? Should it perhaps be two books, or even three?

Do the scenes fall loosely into three groups? If not, should they?

### Notes

1. 'There was an Englishman, and Irishman and a Scotsman . . .'
2. J. Conrad, *Heart of Darkness* (London: Penguin Books, 2000).
3. See R. McKee, *Story* (London: Methuen, 1999), for a fuller explanation of the concept of Active Questions.

4. M. Mitchell, *Gone With The Wind* (London: Macmillan, 1936).
5. N. Hornby, *High Fidelity* (London: Indigo/Gollancz, 1995).
6. Note that in almost all the Bond books the villain is mentioned early in the story but Bond does not actually meet him until around halfway through the book – see the section on 'Length . . .' above.
7. You'll need it.
8. J. R. R. Tolkein, *The Lord of the Rings* (London: Allen and Unwin, 1954).
9. D. Tartt, *The Secret History* (London: Penguin, 1992).
10. T. Berger, *Little Big Man* (New York: Harville, 1999).
11. C. Dickens, *Oliver Twist* (London: PPC, 2004).
12. C. Bronte, *Jane Eyre* (London: Penguin, 1994).
13. M. Twain, *The Adventures of Tom Sawyer* (London: PPC, 2004).
14. J. Conrad, *Heart of Darkness* (New York: Doubleday, 1910).
15. M. Amis, *London Fields* (London: Penguin, 1992).
16. The crucial point here is not that your story has to have a journey, but that if it doesn't then you will need to put something in its place.
17. J. Campbell, *The Hero's Journey* (San Francisco: Harper, 1991). This is a fairly heavy read, though worth the effort. For a summary of Campbell's ideas in more easily digestible form from a writer's point of view, see C. Vogler, *The Writer's Journey* (London: Pan, 1999).
18. L. Carroll, *Alice in Wonderland* (London: PPC, 1994).
19. D. Brown, *The Da Vinci Code* (London: Corgi, 2004).
20. J. Austen, *Pride and Prejudice* (London: OUP, 2004).
21. I. McEwan, *Enduring Love* (London: Vintage, 2004).

# 4

# Making Fiction from Fact, Making Fact of Your Fiction

Graeme Harper

---

## Acts and events

Very rarely, nothing happens. Real and genuine nothing, that is. A nice stretch of nothing might be quite a relief! But it's pretty elusive. Most often what's happening is something. Naturally, not everyone notices all of it, although the bigger things, they're pretty obvious. The spectacular successes, the terrible disasters, the monstrous acts, the mighty achievements: they're noticeable. But how often have you read fiction that is based *only* on these things? Different kinds of fiction have different relationships with what's happening around us, with what we might call 'fact'. That's what this chapter is about.

One generalization might suggest that the more 'literary' fiction often concentrates on the smaller somethings around us and the more 'popular' fiction often concentrates on the bigger somethings. But that, like most generalizations, cuts a lot of corners, and in reality fiction roams over the acts and events of the world with relative free rein.

It's also true that not every type of fiction deals with what we would normally consider to be acts and events. Certainly not with the same sense of them being fundamental. Some fiction appears to be largely static, concentrating instead on impression or attitude, aspect or intention or, to put it another way: some fiction presents a picture rather than a performance.

49

Likewise, some fiction draws more on the factual than others. Historical fiction, to take an entirely obvious example, frequently relies on an accurate depiction of a set of events from the past, and at least part of the reason for its considerable popularity relates to this. Other fiction, the personal story of a relationship or the fantastic story of alien planets, for example, approximates fact through more empathetic means. Whatever type of fiction, in fact, a form of empathy lies at its core.

Because empathy is that condition of being able to identify with, and to an extent understand, the states of mind of others, it's quite obviously at the forefront of the fiction writer's daily work. That is not to say that all good fiction writers are great with other people. Far from it; stories of reclusive, temperamental or just plain difficult writers are well known. That's a different thing. The empathy displayed in fiction is mostly not a kind of advanced fakery either; not in fiction that is well written, anyway. It's more than a writer saying to themselves that if they just use one trick or another then they'll pull in their readers.

Rather, the empathy that informs and generates fiction is a combination of personal and more general fact combined with a desire to communicate in some way. Empathy, it has to be added, is not sympathy. Empathy does not mean that the writer is, by nature, benevolent. Like anyone else, any one writer might be both sympathetic and benevolent but that's not necessarily empathy. Empathy is, by definition, simply about understanding in order to anticipate. In the fiction writer's case, this is anticipation of how readers will react.

It is true of all fiction that one of the key reasons for reading it is because it provides new insights into the world and into ourselves or, alternatively, interestingly develops ones we already had. This said, to be able to captivate a reader, whether through the creation of a short story or of a novel, means thinking about what will offer something fairly unique in return for the effort of reading. Because there is so much of it – something going on, that is – uniqueness, or the ability to be distinctive enough to repay a reader's effort, asks two fundamental things: first, that the writer creates from whatever familiar or discovered information about the world they have a sense of their ability to interpret it well; secondly, that the writer creates from whatever familiar or discovered information about the world they have a sense of their ability to deal with it with empathy.

Writing fiction is not, in essence, weaving something from nothing; rather it is weaving something from something. But from what?

## De-familiar

The ordinary isn't very interesting, though it might well be comfortable. The extraordinary is sometimes breathtaking, but perhaps borders too often on the bizarre. Somewhere between the ordinary and the extraordinary is where most fiction operates. Take these three passages, for example:

> 1. For most of that first winter, I didn't go anywhere. Once, every ten days, I would drive to the Grand Union in Battleboro to shop for food, but that was the only thing I allowed to interrupt my routine.[1]
> 2. Clothed in one of her old nightgowns, my Lolita lay on her side with her back to me, in the middle of the bed. Her lightly veiled body and bare limbs formed a Z. She had pulled both pillows under her dark tousled head; a band of pale light crossed her top vertebrae.[2]
> 3. It was a hundred and fifteen pounds they needed, as well as what was in the box. It was a huge sum, almost so big as to be unreal, not actual money but just sounds in the mouth. Back Home he would never have taken such a step. Not even thought of it.[3]

The word 'defamiliarize' has a relatively specific meaning in literary critical circles, referring, broadly, to technique in the writing arts. The term emerged from the Russian Formalists critics of the early twentieth century who, as their name suggests, were frequently concerned with formal technical experiment by writers, consideration of 'devices' and what was broadly called 'poetic language', even in reference to prose.

But to 'defamiliarize' also has a broader meaning and many use it simply to refer to something that 'makes new' or 'makes unfamiliar' or even, in the very widest sense, 'makes strange'. The ability, then, to defamiliarize is the ability to highlight, perhaps, the innovation that occurs in a piece of writing at the technical, or formal, level; but it also could refer to anything that raises a piece of writing higher in the consciousness of the reader. In other words, something that makes a piece of fiction stand out in the mind of the reader and perhaps, therefore, repay the reader's effort in choosing to read it.

The first extract, above, is from Paul Auster's novel *The Book of Illusions* (2002). The story concerns a grieving college professor who, after having lost his wife and two children in a plane crash, discovers the work of a comedian of silent cinema named Hector Mann, who makes him laugh. Studying Mann's work as a kind of therapeutic activity, he discovers not only that Mann had disappeared after making a relative handful of films; but also that Mann is still alive. It could be said that, in terms of its topic, the book deals with reasonably familiar territory: grief, the life of a teacher, film. But looking even at the micro-level of a few sentences from the novel it can be seen that Auster knows the technique of making even the smallest idea one that can seem intriguing, alluring, even compelling.

'For most of that first winter', Auster's narrator writes, 'I didn't go anywhere.' It might seem a relatively minor point, but the position of the word 'most' and the impact it has in defining the sense of the sentence are notable. If it was only for 'most' and not 'all' the first winter then, at some point, the narrator did go somewhere. Where he went, therefore, is a point of interest. So, the question becomes, 'When you weren't going nowhere, where did you go?' Auster answers that next: 'Once, every ten days, I would drive to the Grand Union in Battleboro to shop for food . . .' So now there is a car journey to something, somewhere, for something. The possibility that on that journey, or because of that journey, something happened is raised. The reader is alerted to this by the specific reference to a type of journey and a place. Auster concludes the idea, for the moment at least, with: '. . . but that was the only thing I allowed to interrupt my routine'. Thus we hear the voice of the narrator; the distinct choice of 'allowed' and 'routine' suggest a certain kind of perspective on a certain kind of act. The rest of the paragraph, building on this groundwork, explores the reason for the narrator's avoidance of traveling and, Auster having set this up, then recalls a moment at which the narrator's planning falls apart and the break in routine produces an unexpected result.

There are many ways in which Auster's passage might be interpreted. And, indeed, as many fiction writers themselves would point out, there is a good chance that Auster didn't entirely orchestrate his prose so consciously as to produce such an intricate maneuver. On the other hand, this is part of the fiction writer's sense of crafting and, equally, no one is saying that the process is always a conscious one, particularly for the experienced writer; nor is anyone suggesting that this sense of creating what could rightly be included under the term 'the de-familiarized' involves more than careful juxtaposition of idea and the writer's general approach to it. To do this well, however, is another matter.

Defamiliarization mostly involves a technique often mentioned alongside it, called 'foregrounding'. Foregrounding, or making something stand out, is essentially the act of distinguishing for the reader what is interesting and unique in the work in front of them. When Vladimir Nabokov writes in the second extract, which comes from his 1959 novel *Lolita*, that 'Her lightly veiled body and bare limbs formed a Z', he has brought to the fore an image, an idea and a point of view that captures the reader's attention and repays that attention with a new insight. Whether the reader agrees with the sexual mores, the personal obsession or the wider approach to life suggested by Nabokov's narrator in *Lolita* is something else. But here, in a simple act of description, the writer has shown his ability to empathize with the reader's keenness to see the world anew, to have it further illuminated. The Z-shaped body beneath the light veil of 'one of her old nightgowns' is not simply, therefore, the narrator's provocation, it is a melding of visionary effects, all of which make us reconsider the image and the idea behind it.

The final extra comes from Kate Grenville's novel *The Secret River* (2005). This is a novel concerned with early Australia and the meeting of European settlers, and transported convicts and the indigenous population. Grenville, the winner of the Orange Prize for Fiction among other awards, builds on the background of her own family history to explore the nature of identity and ownership within the Australian context. It is a story that therefore bases itself in specific national, cultural and personal circumstances but its ideas, themes and subject matter have much greater resonance.

Consider these two snippets of Grenville's prose: '. . . not actual money but just sounds in the mouth' and 'Back Home he would never have taken such a step.' The first shifts money from the observable, logical world to a different plain of reference. Money becomes a sound. What a wonderful conceptual leap! But also a great way of capturing a notion: the notion, in this case, that the sum of money was so large that it was impossible to imagine it as real money at all. In effect, Grenville has brought to the fore the size of the problem, and explained to the reader exactly how unique a problem it is. Indeed, the second snippet adds extra dimension to this; here, Back Home, which is capitalized to emphasize a concept used by settlers, defines a different sense of personal and public action, and the simple phrasing adds to the feeling that the viewpoint used is plainly stating the case. Intricate or descriptive prose is not needed in the final snippet: the difference between Back Home and this new country is intriguing in itself.

In many ways, Grenville, Nabokov and Auster have analyzed, and built on, their personal histories. Nabokov's relationship with his adopted United States has been widely documented and the journey, both physical and metaphorical, that his narrator, Humbert, and his captured obsession, Lolita, make through the heartland of the United States is indicative of the kind of journey Nabokov himself was making from his early Russian home to his new North American one. Themes and subjects are most certainly built around that, but the core of Lolita relates back to Nabokov's own life. In fact, each of the writers here constructs their fiction between the familiar and the new, considering what makes their stories unique and foregrounding this, linking personal knowledge with researched knowledge and balancing the ordinary and the extraordinary.

## The tidal pool

A formal analysis of prose fiction can reveal a writer's technique, and assist other writers in understanding the nature of both the process of building a story or a novel and the final construction itself. But this is only part of the picture. Perspective, or the encouragement of a standpoint that grows a writer's empathetic relationship with their readers, involves more than just a look at formal composition techniques. There are cultural, social, economic and political factors that impact on people's personal standpoints. There are matters of taste and personal preference that involve complex exchanges between psychological factors and more holistic ones. So, in order to develop a sense of what is going to be an enjoyable focus for a piece of fiction, combine personal writer's interest with likely reader's interest. This will, ultimately, prove successful for both writer and reader. It is a multi-layered process. This is one of those areas where it's easier to suggest that there is no rhyme or reason to any of it and therefore nothing much to discuss. But, frankly, that's a bit of a cop out. It's difficult, but not impossible, to see what drives the engine of fiction, much as it is to see what drives poetry or a script.

One straightforward link between technique and perspective is that which involves giving texture to the fictional depiction of everyday experience. If it's true that lives are generally not full of nothing, then it is equally true that large parts of life passes people by. There are psychological and physiological reasons for this connected, not least, with the need to focus on those things that ensure survival. So, for example, it is more likely someone will spend time thinking about ensuring they are fed and clothed than they will spend time contemplating the wonders of a beautiful landscape or an intriguing set of cultural relations. Everyone at some point must focus on the simply pragmatic over the aesthetic or perhaps even life-enriching, and fiction frequently allows back into people's lives those things that the rush of existence does not provide time to enjoy.

An area of keen interest in that regard is the area of memory. Henri Bergson, philosopher and winner of the Nobel Prize for Literature in 1927, talked interestingly about the nature of memory in *Matter and Memory* (1896) and on other topics of interest to writers in such books as *Creative Evolution* (1907), ranging throughout his career over investigations of such things as creativity, time, comedy, consciousness and the nature of existence. Much of this is beyond the scope of discussion here, but at least one element does have relevance for creative writers and that is the idea that Bergson put forward that there are two different kinds of memory. The first, habit memory, is linked to repetition and to sensorimotor functions; in other words, it is essentially part of ordinary bodily perception and determined by fairly accessible aspects of day-to-day human action. The second, however, Bergson talked about as something quite different, labeling it 'pure memory'. This pure memory, according to Bergson, is unconscious and spontaneous: it's the kind of memory that informs dreams and seems to be ordered and arranged not according to the pressures of our day-to-day activities. Though, according to Bergson, this kind of memory is unconscious it is well worth considering how it might be a frequent practical part of the perspective that informs creative writing.

Fiction writing draws down through current and past experience. Like Bergson's concept of the two forms of memory, fiction writing aims to be part of the contemporary reactions and foundations of people's lives, and to provide a gaze into the gaps in the everyday. In that way, a piece fiction can appear much like the depiction of a waking dream and it is easy to see why, in that regard, such people as Sigmund Freud showed an interest in the working lives of creative writers, and perhaps also why Freud described the writer's activities as if they were daydreaming and infantile play.

What Freud missed, and what Bergson saw, was that in order to write creatively – in the case here, to write fiction – the writer is essentially diving down into a tidal pool, endeavoring to be alert to the world beyond habit memory. The analogy is simple: near the surface of the pool is the water we're frequently swimming in, the water we stroke through every day. Now and then from deeper in the pool a current brings other aspects to the surface, previous elements that have sunk further down. Still further, sometimes new things wash in from the ocean of experience beyond us. The different levels of the pool are not separate, and they are largely not able to be controlled; however, once recognized by the writer, they can at least be actively employed.

The trick, then, is for the fiction writer to be able to make the link between perception that might be here and now, memory, that might be brought to the surface from any point in the past and at any time, and new ideas, thoughts and experiences that arrive either expectedly or unexpectedly.

## Possibility

### 'What if?'

This question drives fiction writing. It sets a challenge to a premise, perhaps, or introduces the basis of an argument that will be answered by a fictional exploration. For example, 'What if Atlantis really did exist today?' or 'What if you discovered your sister was an alien?' All 'What if?' questions do not have to be as unlikely as this, but the principle remains the same no matter how ordinary, or outrageous, the rest of the question might be. The essential 'What if?' sets a narrative or a story in motion. This is not to say all fiction is based on story or narrative, but certainly a great deal of it is. The question also asks for contemplation and, based on the writer's empathy and on defamiliarization and foregrounding, presents the reader with the likelihood of seeing things anew, or more thoroughly, than they did before reading the writer's work.

'What if?' is driven by possibility. These simple two words require, and provide, an opportunity to exchange between writer and reader some aspect of human existence. They are also a key way of bridging between the day-to-day aspects of perception and those that are, perhaps, deeper in our pool of experience, thought or feeling.

Thinking and writing in terms of 'What if?' helps to ensure that each page is composed with at least some sense that it is providing a response to something, to someone, for someone. And responsive writing is writing that is aware that each action potentially causes a reaction. In other words, 'What if?' keeps the lines of communication open between writer and reader.

While thinking practically about how to draw upon and use the attitudes of the human memory has been linked to the work of Bergson, perhaps the 'What if?' concept should really link most logically to the work of the scientist Sir Issac Newton. Newton's third law, *The Law of Interaction*, presented as one of his three laws of motion in *Principia Mathematica Philosophiae Naturalis* (1686), suggests that for every action, or force, in nature there's an equal and opposite reaction. If we see writing and reading as natural phenomena, then it is sensible to imagine a 'What if?' reader's reaction to a 'What if?' writer's action.

Reading is certainly a very natural human act: it's only in reading such things as the weather or the facial expressions or body language of others that we can manage the world at all. So it is not out of keeping with this to consider how such laws of natural phenomenon work. It's also a useful guide to recall that in the 'action–reaction' law either element can work as an action or a reaction, and that its forces occur in pairs. There is never, in other words, an action without a reaction.

Newton's other two laws of motion have relevance here too. His first law, *The Law of Inertia*, suggests that an object in motion has a tendency to stay in motion, and an object at rest has a tendency to stay at rest, unless the object is acted upon by an outside force. While Newton's second law, *The Law of Acceleration*, suggests that the acceleration with which an object moves is directly proportional to the magnitude of the force applied to the object, and inversely proportional to the mass of the object.

Thinking analogically, it's easy to imagine what these final two Newtonian laws suggest for fiction. First, that asking 'What if?' sets things in motion, the writer working toward a reaction from the reader. Without a 'What if?', no movement – in whatever way movement is defined, whether in terms of emotional movement, physical or geographic movement, or movement through a set of points on a plot map, to take just a few examples – will occur. Secondly, that there are different paces with which fiction might move forward and thus different magnitudes of 'force' that can be applied – 'force' in this sense meaning such things as the use of grammar (e.g. verbs having more forward movement than nouns) and word choice and syntax (e.g. complex words slowing things down, short sentences often speeding things up). Constant referral to a set of 'What if?' questions might well create fiction that is fast moving but shallow in its examination of the ideas, attitudes or feelings being considered. Infrequent referral to a set of 'What if?' questions might well create fiction that is just about stopped still, dwelling perhaps at too great a length on each element of the fiction, so that the reader is wondering if completing the reading will lead anywhere at all.

Newton's laws are a good reminder that, once set in motion, the interaction between fiction writer and fiction reader relates also to the impact of pace and the way in which points on the timeline from the beginning of the fiction to the end of the fiction are managed. This interaction also relates to the general sense of a texture and shape that likewise is part of the fact that the writing and reading of fiction is the coming together of two different sets of personal actions, two different sets of pure memory and habit memory as Bergson might describe it, part of a 'law of motion' that is guided by humans behaving as generally social, interactive, communicative and creative beings.

## Gym

Many writers write fiction as a form of escape from the everyday; others write it as a mode of open investigation of what is plainly in front of them, sometimes of the ordinary and sometimes of the extraordinary, but most often of things somewhere in between. Others are drawn to fiction by its ability to combine different aspects on knowledge into one more or less speculative package. Part of the process of discovery relates to an investigation of the nooks and crannies of life: essentially building fiction from the something going on all around us, but doing it in a way that provides new insights or provides an opportunity for greater development of already established ones. Writing fiction is an eclectic act, drawing on potentially infinite sites of knowledge, combining them in any number of ways, and producing almost as many versions of 'a piece of fiction' as there are people on the planet to produce it. Nothing is formally outside the realm of fiction, therefore there is the absence of the 'safety net' of a limited field of discourse: where the writer roams on the screen or page, where they take the reader and where the two of them ultimately end up are entirely open.

Of course, all art forms face the same problem, this lack of a fallback position. It's impossible for the artist, in the large part, to declare, 'I didn't go there because it's not where we artists go.'

The journey for artist and their audience is wide open to anything. With this in mind, practicing the arts – the writing arts included – can be both enlivening and frightening at the same time. There is ultimately no absolute to any of it; there are only probabilities and possibilities.

### Exercises

1. Let's start with the works of others. Choose three novels and consider what facts seem to drive them? Are these facts about 'big events' or are they about something else, personal issues, 'micro' elements of life? For example, are these novels constructed around a set of characters whose knowledge of each other, or possible lack of knowledge of each other, drives the engine of the fiction? Alternatively, are these novels more related to a set of historical facts and circumstances that are external to the workings of a relationship or the thoughts of an individual – is it these things that drive the fiction? Or, alternatively still, does the driving force of these fictions appear to be scientific or economic or social fact; are they, in other words, somehow aiming to be representative of the bigger cycles and circumstances of the world?

Compare and contrast each of these three works. Which seems to work better for you, and why? Can you compare them with shorter fiction, three short stories for example, and find similar use of facts, circumstances or attitudes? Can you recognize what might be called the writer's empathetic reading of their audience? That is, what appeal does the writer appear to be making to you as a reader? Do they seem to know, however subtly, something about how you view the world?

Now consider what the relationship might be between your sense of the world as it appears before you, and the world that is envisaged through a meeting of contemporary immediate experience and your memories. Can you imagine a story constructed between observation and memory? Try doing this a few times, consciously. That is, try to construct a few small passages from potentially different stories based on the things that are around you and things that you remember but that are not immediately visible. What's the method of selection you're using to choose the observed things, and to choose the memories to highlight?

Can you see a pattern of a relationship – something perhaps distinct to yourself and your life history and your background?

2. Empathy, as noted, is not necessarily sympathy or benevolence; empathy is a condition of identification, understanding and anticipation. As an exercise, then, construct six passages of fiction – just short passages of, perhaps, 200–400 words each – and consider the kinds of reactions you are expecting from your reader. In many ways, this is something of a simplification of the process, but it does highlight the relationship between the writer's approach to the reader, or action, and the reader's feelings about the writer and their work, or reaction. Sir Isaac Newton would be pleased! Newton's action–reaction law is all about acknowledging that many of the things that happen around us, to us and because of us are the result of exchanges of some sort.

Your six passages might be constructed with the idea that each of them will display a particular kind of emotion or feeling, or encourage a particular emotion or feeling in the reader. So, for example, one passage might aim to show love, another to show desire, a third one to show apprehension. The real test is whether you can construct a passage showing these things without mentioning the words themselves (i.e. love, desire, apprehension)! A second part of the exercise might be to construct passages and ask readers to respond to them, explaining to you how each passage makes them feel, and what thoughts each encourages. Depending on the emotion/feeling attempted, it might be best to duck when asking for a reaction!

3. And, finally, to the Newtonian laws: look at the action–reaction strategy in terms of 'What if?' Set out three scenarios based on 'What if?' and journey along the road of 'What if?' to the point where there seems to be a logical or satisfying end to the set of questions that drive you on. Now take those three scenarios and imagine the method of expanding them constructed at a variety of speeds. Is there some way to speed up, or slow down, the movement through the sequence? Can you imagine points, or answers, that are more important to you to dwell upon than others? Have a close look at the point of inertia and the points of acceleration and think about how managed these seem to be and how natural they might be. Are

you able to adjust these successfully by formal means? If so, what are they?

## Notes

1. P. Auster, *The Book of Illusions* (London: Faber, 2002), p. 70.
2. V. Nakokov, *Lolita* (London: Weidenfeld, 1959), p. 127.
3. K. Grenville, *The Secret River* (Melbourne: Text, 2005), p. 117.

# 5

# Narrative Point of View: Who Tells the Story?

Linda Anderson

## Authors and narrators

A few years ago I gave a reading of one of my stories at a literary festival. The story was about a woman whose child was killed in a motoring accident. I used the first-person point of view: the woman's 'own' voice telling her story as 'I'. The character-narrator was very different from me in appearance, background and life history. But afterwards, two members of the audience came up to commiserate with me about the tragedy I had endured. They looked shocked when I told them that I had never had a child – it was as if I had duped them. Spanish author Javier Marías describes a more intensive experience of a similar kind in his book *Dark Back of Time* (2004 [2003]).[1] He set his novel *All Souls* (2003 [1989]) in Oxford where he had earlier taught at the university for 2 years.[2] He was dismayed when real people, including Oxford dons and antiquarian booksellers, mistook themselves for his fictional characters and confused him with his nameless narrator, 'the Spanish gentleman' (Marías (2004 [2003]: 23). Everything his narrator said was in danger of being ascribed to him personally. One of his first intimations of this happened when a woman student enquired solicitously about his baby. When he replied that he didn't have one, some other students joined in, with the air of being victims of a fraud: 'But you say so in your novel, the one that's just come out' (28).

This kind of absolute identification of an author with the narrator of a piece of fiction is something that can confuse writers as well as readers. Sometimes this occurs when the source material for a story is autobiographical and the writer bases the narrator closely on himself or herself. Even in such a case, the narrator is a fictional version of the author, a constructed persona. Anyone who has ever written an amusing letter while feeling unhappy will recognize the gap between the self who writes and the version that ends up on the page. But the conflation of author and narrator also happens more generally and perhaps one of the reasons is that every new writer is urged to 'find your own voice'. This is an inspiring piece of advice, which encourages writers to value their own experiences, resources and uniqueness. But it does *not* mean that your writing must conform to your habitual modes of utterance. Fiction writers often need to make themselves 'invisible' in order to assume the voices of various characters and narrators. Residual traces of your personal voice may remain but you are free to invent other voices to suit the purposes of your stories. Jack Hodgins in *A Passion for Narrative* explained this process well.[3] He called the writer's own inescapable voice his 'voice-print' and the narrators he takes on his 'voice-masks' (193). With practice, you will be able to impersonate many different narrators to try on many 'masks'.

### Exercise

Try on a voice-mask now. Choose a character who is different from you. You might select a character of the opposite sex or someone dramatically richer or poorer than yourself or someone of a different age. Or you might prefer a character from another era or place or a specific figure, such as a contemporary celebrity. Imagine yourself stepping into the life of this person. Using a first-person point of view (an 'I' tells the story) gives us the thoughts, feelings and perceptions of this character. Write up to 200 words.

The aim of this exercise is to give you the experience of constructing a vivid first-person protagonist telling his or her own story. Many writers find it liberating to create first-person narrators because of the lively, personality-charged voices that emerge. It is also a way of escaping the constraints of 'self' that can sometimes inhibit writing.

You've been experimenting here with first-person narration but writers also use voice-masks when rendering third-person points of view (i.e. telling stories using 'he', 'she' or 'they'). The aim of this chapter is to show you the range of most commonly used points of view and to encourage you to experiment with them so that, with practice, you can make conscious and versatile choices in your own stories or novels.

## The impact of narrative point of view

Every story is just one version of itself. It could always be told in a number of other ways. For example, you might centre the narrative in the consciousness of a secondary character who witnesses events rather than in the mind and feelings of a main character. Or you might use the point of view of an anonymous observer who reports events without offering interpretations. You might prefer a more partisan storytelling voice, a narrator who knows everything and who likes to offer opinions and verdicts. But is there a best way to tell any particular story?

Sometimes writers make this decision intuitively. Perhaps there is one character whose personality or dilemma appeals to you most and it seems right to use his or her perspective. Maybe you start imagining a particular voice and follow that. Very often this strategy pays off but it is also true that writers can get attached to a particular point of view and use it habitually. When I started writing, I would automatically go for a third-person subjective voice, that is using 'he' or 'she' but telling the story intimately from that character's perspective. I loved the paradoxical combination of intense privacy and impersonality that this point of view can yield. But I had a narrow repertoire, almost a 'default mode' of narrative method. Then I happened to read a novel about a timorous character, which was told in the first person. The way this 'boring' character-narrator described her eventless life was compelling. There was something about her confiding tone, her sharp analysis and her desire to break out of her diffidence that made me feel hooked. So I became excited about the power of first-person narration and began to try it out for myself, immediately increasing my sense of choice and control in my writing. My experience as both writer and teacher has convinced me that mastering the basic techniques used to create points of view is the most empowering thing a fiction writer can learn.

To demonstrate the impact of point of view, I've devised four versions of the 'same' fictional material. The shared scenario is that a disappointed father dreads his daughter's forthcoming marriage to a much older man. While you read, think about the following questions:

- Who is telling the story in each version?
- How much knowledge does the teller have?

### Version 1

You should see my soon-to-be son-in-law. He's remarkable, or so Bethany keeps telling me in the edge-of-tantrum voice she uses when I'm being 'unreasonable'. *'Oh Da-aad!'*

She's right, he is remarkable, remarkably 'mature' with polar white hair and a groove in his brow so deep you could plant seeds. He has a remarkable tally of ex-wives, one dead and two divorced, and numerous adult offspring. Even his sons are too old for my daughter.

What on earth can she see in him? Is it the old-fashioned gallantry? Is she bowled over by his minor fame? He's an actor, by the way. You might possibly recognize his face but not be able to put a name to him. The age difference hardly seems to embarrass the arrogant git. When he came to 'meet-the-parents', it was me and Maggie who acted all panicky and shifty, spilling wine and laughing at non-jokes. I even saw him sizing Maggie up, giving her the once-over with his damp bluebeardy eyes.

That first-meeting ordeal is nothing compared to the upcoming nuptials. I'm expected to put on a tux and give away my only daughter to a man old enough to be older than her father. Feeling so robbed, to stand there and give the girl away.

You will recognize this as a *first-person* point of view in the voice of the father (an 'I' tells the story). The voice draws us in by confiding in us, creating a feeling of intimacy and authenticity. This is achieved by a direct address to the reader and by using a tone which is both passionate and conversational: for example, 'the arrogant git' and 'He's an actor, by the way.' We see the situation through the narrator's eyes and get a powerful sense of his character and his predicament. The teller knows only what he himself is capable of knowing, thinking or discerning.

### How is it done?

First-person narration is the most straightforward storytelling technique because access to the character's thoughts is smooth and immediate, without the filter of another narrating voice. You can create a vivid sense of individuality by using the character's personal voice including any special mannerisms such as slang, favourite sayings, faulty grammar or colloquial language as appropriate.

### Version 2

Richard sits at his desk shuffling photographs of his daughter, trying to remember if he has ever been sadder. The pictures are like a ticker-tape of small triumphs – Bethany getting her degree, Bethany brandishing the key to her first car, Bethany enjoying her twenty-first birthday party, surrounded by friends. Including eligible young men, Richard notices, wishing he had encouraged one of them, any of them, to pursue his daughter. He would bribe one of them now except for fear of looking deranged.

Maybe it was all his fault, the fact that Bethany was about to marry an old goat? Perhaps he hadn't been fatherly enough and that was why she felt drawn to the suave wrinkly with the wavy white hair like whipped cream? He wonders if he should have opposed the marriage more fiercely, not given in? But Bethany's threats were so cruel. 'I'll never have any contact with you ever again!' She expects him to feign happiness on her wedding day, to make a traditional speech. What on earth can he say? Welcome, sir, into my family. We don't mind adding to your vast collection.

Although this version is written in the third person (i.e. the writer uses 'he', 'she' or 'they'), it also delivers an intimate sense of the character's subjectivity. It uses a *third-person limited omniscient* point of view, which means that the narrator knows everything that the character may see, feel and know but knows nothing more about other protagonists or events than the chosen character. This technique is also sometimes known as 'single character point of view' because the author allows us to see the world through the perspective of the chosen character.

### How is it done?

An anonymous narrator reports everything from the chosen character's perspective, conveying his or her inner thoughts as well as observing the character's behaviour from the outside. This creates intimacy but with a certain degree of distance because of the shadowy presence of the narrator organizing and commenting on the story. Part of the sense of intimacy comes from the relationship created between narrator, character and reader. It is as if the narrator and the reader are confidants. The technique combines the chosen character's personal voice and the hidden narrator's reporting of that in 'free indirect style', a fusion of third- and first-person perspectives first developed at the end of the eighteenth century. In free indirect style, a direct thought, such as 'Maybe it's all my fault, the fact that Bethany's about to marry an old goat', is transposed into the third person and the past tense: 'Maybe it was all his fault that Bethany was about to marry an old goat.' Occasionally direct thoughts can occur without tags such as 'he thinks' or 'he wonders', as in the conclusion of this version: 'Welcome, sir into my family. We don't mind adding to your vast collection.'

### Version 3

> It is the saddest night of Richard's life, or so he feels. He has struggled to write the speech he must make at his daughter's wedding but nothing occurs to him except envenomed little jokes. Thank you, Bethany, for finding someone who makes me feel positively junior. Adam, I hope your pension plan will take care of my daughter's student loans.
>
> It is possible that no bridegroom would have pleased Richard Brook. No one good enough for the golden girl who has never before given him sleepless nights. Beautiful Bethany, merry and healthy, no bad grades, no pregnancy scares, no brushes with the law, not even a tattoo. Richard and his wife Maggie are fond of talking about how they have always been 'friends' to their daughter, who they claimed was unbelievably wise and articulate from an early age. They created a tight little trio of co-equals who delighted in each other and had very little conflict. In effect, they banished the age difference between parents and child. Now they can't bear Bethany's indifference to this other age gap. They also can't see that they have encouraged their daughter to bypass youth and rebellion. She wants the shelter of another adoring 'father'.

This is an example of *third-person omniscient* point of view. An omniscient narrator can enter the consciousness of any character; know the thoughts, histories and motivations of all the characters, including things they may not know themselves; know what has happened elsewhere or in the past and what will happen in the future; intervene in the narrative to comment on the action, issue forewarnings of future events or offer philosophical reflections on life.

Throughout this version, we are aware of the narrator presiding over the story and controlling its telling. In the opening sentence, we see the narrator pulling back from Richard's emotional assessment of the situation in that little doubt-casting phrase 'or so he feels'. The piece is full of analysis and interpretation, 'telling' rather than 'showing' (although in a longer piece, there would be a balance of scenes and summarizing). The narrator knows and declares things that Richard may not fully suspect – that he and his wife have contributed to their current dilemma by the way they have raised their daughter. The language is formal and dispassionate but the narrator's attitude can be deduced from an ironic tone in certain words and phrases such as 'golden girl' and 'tight little trio'.

Third-person omniscience was a popular choice in nineteenth-century novels such as those by Fyodor Dostoevsky, Jane Austen and George Eliot. It became unfashionable as discoveries in psychology and science throughout the twentieth century eroded belief in the possibility of absolute 'truth' and impartiality. But omniscience appears to be making a comeback in literary fiction and also remains a standard method for certain 'genre' narratives, like science fiction. If you like the idea of using a third-person narrator with a distinctive personality who has a lot to say about a particular theme or period of time, omniscience could be the right choice for some of your stories.

*How is it done?*

Unlimited powers are hard to handle, so the main thing to say is that it needs to be done with great awareness of your purpose in any given story. Just because you have the ability to enter the consciousness of every character, it doesn't mean that you are obliged to do so. There will be more details later about how to handle omniscient viewpoints with clarity and consistency.

## Version 4

It is late at night in the Brook household after the first visit of Bethany Brook's fiancé. She and her father are sitting opposite each other, finishing off a bottle of wine at a table strewn with the detritus of a big meal. Bethany's eyes and lips gleam in the candlelight. She smiles momentarily before breaking the silence.

'So, you got on well, didn't you?'

'I guess,' her father sighs. 'We are near contemporaries, after all. Lots in common.'

'Oh, he gets on with everyone.'

'He's a charmer all right.'

'And so handsome with it.' Bethany hugs herself.

'Yes, all his own teeth and a full head of hair.'

'Go on, admit it, you were well impressed.'

Richard plays with some crumbs on the table, rounding them up. 'I watched you both from the window, you know, when you were arriving. You walked up the path without touching. He looked like your probation officer.'

'We were nervous. Anyway, would you have preferred it if we had looked like lovers?'

Richard lifts a crumpled napkin and twists it. 'Nervous, you say. He showed no nerves. Consummate actor, obviously.'

'Dad, I know why you're worried. Because when I'm forty, he'll be . . . But all we care about is now. Now is all that matters. That's what you always taught me.'

This version is written in the *third-person objective* point of view. This viewpoint is impersonal. The narrator is confined to recording what may be witnessed from external facts and appearances. He or she will not enter the characters' thoughts or give any interpretations or judgements. As with film, everything must be inferred from gestures, expressions, actions, dialogue and silences.

*How is it done?*

Without access to the characters' thoughts and feelings, how can we tell what they are thinking? The way it works is that what has been left out of the story still haunts it. What the characters say hints at what they cannot utter. Let's scrutinize this version in detail and try to interpret each small gesture and line of dialogue. I'll repeat the story here with inserted notes tracking what's going on underneath its quiet surface.

> It is late at night in the Brook household after the first visit of Bethany Brook's fiancé. She and her father are sitting opposite each other, finishing off a bottle of wine at a table strewn with the detritus of a big meal. Bethany's eyes and lips gleam in the candlelight (*brief scene-setting*). She smiles momentarily (*indicating nervousness and determination*) before breaking the silence.
>
> 'So, you got on well, didn't you?' (*direct confrontation but with a pleading quality*).
>
> 'I guess,' her father sighs. (*reveals sadness, perhaps a degree of resignation*). 'We are near contemporaries, after all. Lots in common.' (*takes the opportunity to allude to the suitor's advanced age*).
>
> 'Oh, he gets on with everyone.' (*deflects insult and takes opportunity to praise her man*).
>
> 'He's a charmer all right.' (*undermines her tribute with sarcastic agreement. Hint of genuine suspicion too*).
>
> 'And so handsome with it.' Bethany hugs herself. (*ignores implied criticism and praises her man even more. Hugs herself in a gesture that could be gleeful or self-comforting or a bit of both*).
>
> 'Yes, all his own teeth and a full head of hair.' (*another salvo regarding the man's age*).
>
> 'Go on, admit it, you were well impressed.' (*adopts a playful coaxing tone but comes across as slightly beseeching*).

Richard plays with some crumbs on the table, rounding them up. (*'displacement activity' indicating anxiety as he makes his biggest speech so far*).[4] 'I watched you both from the window, you know, when you were arriving. You walked up the path without touching. He looked like your probation officer.' (*adopts an authoritative style as if laying out evidence*).

'We were nervous. Anyway, would you have preferred it if we had looked like lovers?' (*defensive at first but then defiant*).

Richard lifts a crumpled napkin and twists it. (*gesture reveals anxiety and anger*). 'Nervous, you say. He showed no nerves. Consummate actor, obviously.' (*bypasses her question and takes another swipe at the suitor*).

'Dad, I know why you're worried. (*ignores jibe and acknowledges validity of his feelings*). Because when I'm forty, he'll be . . . (*inability to say the word indicates fear and denial*). But all we care about is now. (*powerful switch from 'I' to 'we'*). Now is all that matters. (*powerful rhetorical repetition of 'now'*). That's what you always taught me.' (*springs the perfect trap – how will he get out of that one?*).

By bringing the submerged part of the story to the surface, I've produced this bloated version almost double the size of the original. This gives some idea of the condensed, pared down quality of this kind of story. It also makes visible the kind of relationship an objective narration creates with the reader. The reader has to enter the story imaginatively and do a lot of intuitive work. Your own interpretation of the story and your speculations about the underlying emotions of the characters may differ from mine. With a story like this, each reader fills in the gaps for themselves and some things remain ambiguous.

## Exercises

1. Having looked at these four different ways of spinning a story, you may already have ideas about which ones appeal to you and might suit the stories you have in mind. Try out these four methods now for yourself. Imagine a conflict between two characters. A teacher opposes a colleague's attitudes towards educating children; an elderly woman resists her son's desire to place her in a nursing home; a young man in love competes with a rival for a girl. Or invent your own scenario.

2. Write about the situation four times from the four different points of view outlined in this chapter, using up to 200 words for each version.

3. When you have completed your four versions, make notes to yourself about the experience. Can you identify where your

strengths lie? Did you enjoy presenting the workings of your main character's mind? Or did you prefer to keep the reader at a greater distance? Did you enjoy the constraints of any particular method or feel rebellious about any of them? Were you surprised by your response to any of the methods? Which version works best for you and your story and why? You might like to develop your favourite version into a completed story.

## Handling point(s) of view in novels

A novel may be told very successfully by one narrator but novelists often like to use multiple narrators in order to explore several characters and show many facets of a story. In the *shifting first-person method*, two or more first-person narrators take turns to tell the story. The presentation of more than one version of events counteracts the inevitable partiality of a single account. It also involves the readers intimately: their sympathies and allegiances may chop and change as the story progresses. It's a method that demands a lot of virtuosity on the part of the writer, who has to create a distinctive and compelling voice for each narrator. Here are a couple of brief examples from two of the four narrators in Andrea Levy's *Small Island*, which explores racist attitudes in post-war England:[5]

Gilbert:
My mirror spoke to me. It said: 'Man, women gonna fall at your feet.' In my uniform of blue – from the left, from the right, from behind – I looked like a god. And the uniform did not even fit me so well. But what is a little bagging on the waist and tightness under the arm when you are a gallant member of the British Royal Air Force? (105)

Queenie:
In Herefordshire, Hertfordshire and Hampshire hurricanes hardly ever happen. My elocution teacher said the problem was that my mouth was too quick to stretch into a smile when I spoke. 'You'll never get on in polite society like that, Miss Buxton.' Tulip, dandelion, buttercup – I said them all wrong. Bottle, cup, saucer were not much better. My mouth was too weak, it needed discipline and Mrs Waterfall was the woman to give it. (206)

The voices are beguiling, convincing and utterly different.

The *shifting third-person method* is also a popular strategy with contemporary novelists. Third-person limited viewpoints are used and each shift is signalled by a subtle but definite change of tone or register. For example, Maggie Gee's epic novel *The Flood*, about a city threatened by ever-rising waters, features a very large number of viewpoint characters.[6] Here is the way that three of them are introduced in the opening pages of the novel:

> May stood at the window, smiling at the street, the narrow impoverished street she loved, and thought, thank you God for small mercies. The rains have ended. I've got children; life goes on, and I'm still here. She put on a kettle, and made some tea. (11–12)
>
> Lottie loved light, and the day was alight. The morning poured in, glorious, between the curtains she never closed. Lottie heard birds, though she didn't know which ones – if only Harold were awake, she could ask him – and she lifted her head and glimpsed blossom outside, bobbing blossom in February, Japanese something, Harold had said, scarlet flowers with golden centres, Japanese Quince, for the whole world was connected, red cups blazing on black leafless branches, glorious against the blue. (15)
>
> Bruno knows the end is coming. 'The last days,' Bruno Janes intones. 'The last days, in these last days . . .' He has the gents to himself, this morning. It is kept very clean, with a dark steel mirror which makes him look stronger, more certain than ever. (17)

Notice how the language changes to attune to each different character: May, the homely mother; Lottie, the spoilt, sexy optimist; Bruno, the menacing fanatic.

## Consistency of point of view

Whichever point of view you choose, you need to make sure that you use it consistently. For example, a first-person narrator has to be in a position to know or discover the whole story. Third-person omniscience is the point of view which writers find hardest to control because it is so capacious and wide-ranging. Some omniscient narrations are marred by a constant flitting back and forth from mind to mind, as in the following invented example:

> It was stuffy in the taxi. Bethany was so nervous at the prospect of her parents meeting Adam, that she could not utter a word. She worried that he might be annoyed at her silence but he was grateful as it gave him a chance to calm himself. The taxi driver stole glances at the couple in his mirror, sure he had seen the man somewhere before. Not the girl, though. He would definitely have remembered a stunner like her.

We start with Bethany as the focalized character but suddenly veer into Adam's viewpoint in mid-sentence.[7] We stay with him for a moment before flitting into the taxi-driver's head. This kind of writing irritates and baffles readers. We don't know who is steering the narrative or where to pay attention. For example, is the taxi-driver going to be an important character or is he just going to disappear from the story?

The way to make this example clear and consistent is to lock in to one observing mind. Here it is again from Bethany's viewpoint. Notice how you can still convey similar information:

> It was stuffy in the taxi. Bethany was so nervous at the prospect of her parents meeting Adam, that she could not utter a word. She worried that Adam might be annoyed at her silence but he looked surprisingly composed, not even bothered by the inquisitive taxi-driver who kept eyeing them in his mirror.

## Choosing a point of view

Let's return to the question I posed near the beginning of this chapter. Is there a best way to tell any particular story? How do you know if you have found it?

There is no simple rule about this. Ultimately, the best way will be the one that produces the impact and information that you want to get across in a voice and style that feels unforced. Sometimes this might involve some trial and error though hopefully not on the scale experienced by American author John Irving with his novel *Until I Find You* (2005).[8] At over 800 pages, this is Irving's longest book and his most autobiographical novel to date. It tells the life story of movie actor Jack Burns and his search for his lost father. Irving spent years writing the novel in the first person. When he had finished it, his publishers at Random House loved it and made him an offer, which he accepted. Two days later he decided that this first-person novel should be in the third person and demanded it back. This is how he described the rewriting process:

> Between April of last year, and the end of October, I literally rewrote every sentence from the first to the third-person voice. And that isn't as easy as changing "I" to "he" or "me" to "him". Because often when you change the voice, the tense changes. I found it interesting that there were some elements of the first person, the personal content of it, that you could still keep, but they had a different strength, or a different weight, in a third-person voice. They stood out more.[9]

The original version must have been valid and effective or the publishers would never have bought it. But finally John Irving realized that in this particular story he wanted to capture both the inside and the outside views of his main character; to keep the personal voice but at the slight distance provided by an anonymous narrator. And this is what it comes down to in the end. The writer makes the judgement call. You go with what feels right.

## Notes

1. J. Marías, *Dark Back of Time*, trans. E. Allen (London: Vintage, 2004 [2003]).
2. J. Marías, *All Souls*, trans. M. J. Costa (London: Vintage, 2003 [1989]).
3. J. Hodgins, *A Passion for Narrative: A Guide for Writing Fiction* (New York: St Martin's Press, 1994 [1993]).
4. A psychological term referring to the disguising of emotional feelings by unconscious transference from one object to another. Displacement activities include all kinds of fiddling, distracting behaviours such as foot-tapping, hair-twisting, counting things unnecessarily, whistling and so on.
5. A. Levy, *Small Island* (London: Review, 2004).
6. M. Gee, *The Flood* (London: Saqi Books, 2004).
7. The term 'focalization' was coined by French literary theorist Gerard Genette and is an alternative expression for 'point of view'. It refers to the way that a third-person narrative sees the world from one character's position – a focalized character is the focus of the narrator's attention and will show that character's thoughts.
8. J. Irving, *Until I Find You* (London: Bloomsbury, 2005).
9. L. Black, 'Full Body: John Irving on his job and the upcoming "Until I Find You"', *The Austin Chronicle*, 25th February 2005 (austinchronicle.com).

# 6

# The Journey A Poem Makes

Theodore Deppe

## Introduction

There is, of course, no single way to write a poem, but *the journey* is a suggestive metaphor for how a poem can unfold. Many good poems end up in quite different places than where they began: the writer discovers something she didn't know she felt about her subject, or – as the poem moves down the page – the true subject reveals itself to the poet and the reader.

There are countless reasons to undertake journeys: a tourist heads for an amusement park to have fun; a mourner journeys to his home town to bury a friend; a businesswoman flies to London to close a deal. But the traveller who interests me most is the one who sets off, with a fluid itinerary and an open mind, to see the world and learn about himself.

Fine poems can be written that do no more than express the poet's feelings, but the model I'm describing is one of self-discovery. This is because poems can be precision tools that help us better understand our lives.

This chapter will prepare the writer for the journey and examine how a poem can end up in a place so right that it surprises even the poet. How does one find such a place? Herman Melville cautions, 'It is not down in any map; true places never are.'[1]

## How a poem can happen

Here's a short poem by Eamon Grennan:

> 'Detail'
> I was watching a robin fly after a finch – the smaller bird
> chirping with excitement, the bigger, its breast blazing, silent
> in light-winged earnest chase – when, out of nowhere
> over the chimneys and the shivering front gardens,
> flashes a sparrowhawk headlong, a light brown burn
> scorching the air from which it simply plucks
> like a ripe fruit the stopped robin, whose two or three
> *cheeps* of terminal surprise twinkle in the silence
> closing over the empty street when the birds have gone
> about their own business, and I began to understand
> how a poem can happen: you have your eye on a small
> elusive detail, pursuing its music, when a terrible truth
> strikes and your heart cries out, being carried off.[2]

When I first heard Grennan read 'Detail' at a poetry festival in Galway, it seemed the perfect poem with which to begin that autumn's creative writing class. A colleague of mine had asked Grennan for a copy of the then unpublished poem, so before my first lecture I had my friend read 'Detail' to me over the phone. Reading the lines back to him, I'd just reached 'a light brown bird/scorching the air...' when my friend said, 'No, no, no! It's "a light brown *burn*/scorching the air..."'. And *I* began to understand how a poem can happen. The poet thinks he knows what he's about to say, and suddenly another image – another truth – suggests itself and he follows.

Since the poet was describing a robin, a finch and a sparrow hawk, I thought he was going to write 'a light brown bird' (perhaps Grennan, beginning that sentence, thought the same thing), but 'a light brown burn' is vivid, surprising and right. Similarly, I imagine Grennan had no idea he was going to write an *ars poetica* when he began to describe the tumult he'd witnessed in the sky. 'Detail' is a poem that makes a significant journey and finds its true subject as it unfolds.

On a smaller scale, because the poem is written with only one full stop, it also demonstrates the journey a *sentence* can make; the sentence, too, can begin one place and end somewhere else that is both fitting and unexpected.

Furthermore, my experience listening to 'Detail' over the phone suggests that a poem can also make journeys on the level of the *word*:

instead of settling for the obvious choice, a writer needs to be open to the surprising but right word. 'Bird' becomes 'burn' because the poet's mind is open to lateral travel.

## Exercise

Write a one-sentence poem that begins with something that surprised you recently. This 'something' might simply be a word, or it may be something more dramatic. Let the sentence take a journey: start off with one subject and find your 'true subject' along the way.

### Preparing for the journey

Poems are called into being by other poems. We write because we read. Note that the exercise I've proposed is modelled on Grennan's poem. I'm asking you to imitate. Many young writers are so obsessed with being original that they resist the idea of imitation, but that's like infants refusing to imitate the way their parents walk or talk. We learn to dance, to play violin, to paint by imitating those who do these things well, and writing is no different.

The best preparation for writing is to 'read as a writer'. When you find a poem you like, ask yourself *why* you like it. What strategies and techniques can you learn from the poem?

If you spent a lifetime imitating Grennan, you'd discover many important lessons about writing, but there would always be a derivative feel to your work. However, if you learn from Grennan, then imitate, say, Allen Ginsberg, George Herbert and Carol Ann Duffy, you'll find it impossible to sound like *all* these poets at once. You'll learn strategies from each writer, and how you combine them in your own way will become what's original in your style. As Eudora Welty said, 'For all I know, writing comes out of a superior devotion to reading.'[3] Read the classics as well as your contemporaries. Read widely: philosophy, science, music theory, popular mechanics magazines, the lives of the saints and advice-to-the-lonely newspaper columns.

Meanwhile, pay attention to everything. Henry James said, 'Try to be one of the people on whom nothing is lost.'[4] When people do things that surprise you, make notes. When you laugh inappropriately, ask yourself what prompted your response. These cues might be the beginning of your next journey.

Then, one way or another, make time to write. Remember, the world doesn't *want* you to write. There will always be bills to pay, family to take care of, jobs to get up for, friends to visit, films to watch and so on, endlessly. If you are going to write, make the time and write. If you are tempted to lament your lack of time, think of William Carlos Williams, a prolific writer who was also a busy physician; he'd turn to his typewriter and type a few minutes between patients, then go home and revise the most promising piece each night.

## Packing: What's most important?

Suppose you read the suggested exercise on the last page and couldn't figure out how to begin. The blank page stared back at you. Confronted with nothingness, you elected to pass.

As Adam Zagajewski notes in his essay 'Flamenco', the problem isn't that we have nothing to write about; on the contrary, we have *everything* to write about.[5] Anything we've ever seen, heard or imagined could become a subject. The trick is to find what most needs to be written about. And, as Grennan's poem suggests, we might not discover our true subject until we start writing. Since everything connects, follow your writing wherever it goes and your subconscious will lead to what's most urgent in you. When in doubt, take the path with the most energy.

The rough drafts of Elizabeth Bishop's villanelle 'One Art' reveal how she engaged in something akin to 'free writing' to find her true subject.[6] The first draft mentions that she often loses things; she notes that she misplaces her reading glasses two or three times a day. The second draft rambles down the page, listing everything she's prone to lose. Only after a page of uninspired writing ('This is by way of introduction. I really want to introduce myself. I am such a fantastically good at losing things. I think everyone should profit from my experiences...') does she stumble upon her true subject: the loss of her lover. I call this writing 'uninspired' with a measure of gratitude: if a consummate artist like Bishop can write such a dreadful rough draft, then there's hope for the rest of us. But of course, this is also an example of an absolutely inspired rough draft: she's reckless enough to find her true subject as she careens down the page. There's no hint of what's at stake in this poem as she begins; only in the process of writing does she come upon her true subject. Like the woman in E.M. Forster, Bishop might have said, 'How can I tell what I think till I see what I say?'[7]

## Exercise

Make a quick list of your bad habits, then choose one of them. Write about it for 10 minutes without stopping. Don't worry about punctuation or spelling, and don't worry about being reasonable. After 10 minutes, read what you've written and see whether a line or two might be worth using to begin a second draft. Write for another 10 minutes, still associating freely, and see where you end up. If you have found something worth pursuing, begin to tighten things up in the third draft.

### On not overplanning

For the sort of poem I'm advocating, staying open to where the poem wants to go is crucial. We may think we want to express our views on child abuse, global warming, alcoholism or rape, but often our readers will largely agree with us from the start. When you already know what you want to say, it may be better to write a letter to the editor of your newspaper. In poems, it's often best to surprise ourselves. As Robert Frost remarked, 'No surprise for the writer, no surprise for the reader. For me the initial delight is in the surprise of remembering something I didn't know I knew.'[8]

This strategy of self-discovery is equally true in fiction and drama. The novelist Flannery O'Connor wrote,

> If you start with a real personality, a real character, then something is bound to happen; and you don't have to know what before you begin. In fact it may be better if you don't know what before you begin.
> You ought to be able to discover something from your stories. If you don't, probably nobody else will.[9]

Frost said much the same thing: 'I have never started a poem yet whose end I knew. Writing a poem is discovering.'[10] He also came up with my favourite image of the writing process: 'Like a piece of ice on a hot stove, a poem must ride on its own melting.'[11]

But if you are to follow your imagination, what happens when your mind surprises you with something that never happened? There's no cut-and-dried answer. Sometimes it is best to stick with the facts; sometimes the poem is better if we make things up. Remember, though, we are writing poetry, not autobiography. A poet's final allegiance, perhaps, should be to the poem, not the literal facts. It's crucial to tell the emotional truth, less imperative that we stick to 'what really happened'. The poet Tess Gallagher warns against 'the overaccreditation of the real' – if we insist on describing everything that actually took place, we may bore our readers in the same way tourists do when they subject their extended families to every photo they took on their trip.[12] Like novelists and playwrights, we are making a work of art, and even if we only use what happened, we are choosing details, selecting a point of view, leaving some things out and including others, shaping reality. 'Art is the lie that tells the truth', said Picasso.[13]

Even the Confessionalists – poets like Robert Lowell, Sylvia Plath and Anne Sexton who seem to be telling us exactly what happened in their lives – made some things up. We need to have one foot in this world and one foot in the imagination. Pablo Neruda said, 'The poet who is not a realist is dead. The poet who is only a realist is also dead.'[14]

## Exercise

Describe in detail an incident that really happened to you. Now, introduce a character who was not present in the real-life situation. See what happens when autobiography and fiction meet. Play around with the idea that you can make things up that are still true.

### The art of getting lost

Bishop's drafts for 'One Art' suggest that you might find your true subject by getting lost first. Another poem that provides a useful model for this is Frost's 'Directive'.[15] This journey poem begins with a line that seems intent on confounding the reader: 'Back out of all this now too much for us . . .'. Indeed, he posits a guide 'Who only has at heart your getting lost . . .'. This guide leads the reader to:

> a house that is no more a house
> Upon a farm that is no more a farm
> And in a town that is no more a town . . .

Few poems are so explicit about their intentions: the speaker hopes to get the reader 'lost enough to find yourself'. Then, at journey's end, we come upon a cellar hole of what once was a house, and a brook that supplied water for the home, and 'A broken drinking goblet like the Grail' from which the reader is urged to 'Drink and be whole again beyond confusion'. By undercutting himself throughout, Frost is able to take us on a journey back to our sources.

This business of 'getting lost' runs counter to the premium we put on logical, linear thinking, but any field of creative thought understands its value. Here's the Japanese mathematician Goro Shimura, speaking about a colleague:

> Taniyama was not a very careful person as a mathematician. He made a lot of mistakes, but he made mistakes in a good direction, and so eventually he got right answers, and I tried to imitate him. But I found that it is very difficult to make good mistakes.[16]

Make good mistakes, get lost, say something you didn't know you knew. All these things are difficult. Yet we cannot will the next poem into being; concepts of the muse, inspiration and genius arise because a work of art is not, finally, reducible to planning and hard work. In fact, too much planning, too much plotting, can make a poem seem 'overmediated' and unconvincing.

This is not to say that the poet should eschew reason, logic and hard work. Nor am I advocating that artists should be deliberately obscure. The writer who seeks to approach the inexpressible mystery of things is endlessly interesting, but spare us from those who – by being intentionally unclear – hope we will mistake them for geniuses.

I admire the poems of Jean Valentine, a writer who pays close attention to the movement of dreams. I would find it hard to paraphrase exactly what happens in many of her poems, though they move me deeply. A few years ago, she gave a reading for my students in a high school for the arts, and they all 'got' her. The same evening, she read for my university students, but one of them was troubled by the 'difficult' nature of her poems. Finally, he raised his hand and asked, 'Ms. Valentine, don't you *want* us to understand your work?'. She said at once, 'Oh, yes, definitely, poetry needs to communicate with the reader. I try to make my poems as clear as possible without losing the poem.'

Don't overplan or overexplain, but also don't be deliberately obscure. That sounds easy enough, but each time out you'll find you have to decide how much or how little to say in a poem. In workshops, you'll be told many times to 'Trust the reader', but you'll also be urged to 'Give us a few clues' so that readers can make sense out of things. Charles Wright suggests the writer strive for a 'meticulous abandon'.[17] That sounds about right. Be as clear, precise and detailed as possible as you parachute into the unknown.

## Travelling at the speed of a poem

Many people don't like being surprised when they travel, and they certainly wouldn't like to get lost repeatedly on vacation. Tourists pay large sums of money to companies that do all the planning, hurry them about on a bus, and make sure they see the expected sights. Herded along by the right tour company, you're practically guaranteed that nothing unexpected will happen. You'll return home with digital photos that reproduce all the clichés of travelling in that particular country.

There's nothing (terribly) wrong if you enjoy a packaged holiday, but it is not a useful model for poets to imitate. Instead of a tour bus, the poet-traveller might decide to go, metaphorically, on foot or bicycle, making sure he or she is moving slowly enough to experience the country detail by detail. I once asked Sandra McPherson what was the most important thing she learned from studying with Elizabeth Bishop. She answered, 'Even the details have details.'

This business of slowing down is important in poetry. I think of line breaks as little speed bumps, designed to keep the reader from racing through a poem as if it were a news story. Line breaks can emphasize particular images and bring out the music of words.

In his novel *Slowness*, Milan Kundera notes how we speed up when we want to forget something and slow down, or even stop completely, when we are trying to remember.[18] Poetry, properly heard and understood, must be read out loud, meaning we can't speed-read through it. In the sort of journey I'm advocating, time isn't carefully planned out: one can venture off the beaten track, taste the local wines, open oneself to new experiences, slow down. Sure, there are times to take the *autobahn* or a jet, jump cutting from one scene in a poem to another, but in the type of poem I'm arguing for, there is time to saunter a bit, too.

'Sauntering' is a wonderful word. Thoreau, in his essay 'Walking', claims the word originated in the Middle Ages when beggars claimed to be knights on their way to the Crusades.[19] The children mocked them, crying out, 'There goes a *Sante-Terrer*', another Holy Lander (592). Thoreau says that walkers who do not seek the Holy Land are 'indeed mere idlers and vagabonds, but they who do go there are saunterers in the good sense' (593).

Let's assume you're lucky enough to have found one of those 'true places' that Melville says aren't on any map. You'll probably want to linger there, inhabiting the page fully enough so your reader will be able to saunter inside the poem and use their five senses to experience it, too.

On the other hand, poetry usually succeeds through compression, so one needs to know when to linger, when to move quickly. Larry Levis' poem 'Winter Stars' provides a look at how a gifted poet controls pacing.[20] The poem opens *in medias res*:

> My father once broke a man's hand
> Over the exhaust pipe of a John Deere tractor. The man,
> Ruben Vasquez, wanted to kill his own father
> With a sharpened fruit knife, & he held
> The curved tip of it, lightly, between his first
> Two fingers, so it could slash
> Horizontally, & with surprising grace,
> Across a throat. It was like a glinting beak in a hand,
> And, for a moment, the light held still
> On those vines.

Levis is able to present this moment so vividly for the reader that he can make time stand still, or at least slow it down so that nine and a half lines record what happened in an instant. 'Even the details have details.' Then, in the next three lines, he fast-forwards through the rest of the afternoon:

> When it was over,
> My father simply went in & ate lunch, & then, as always,
> Lay alone in the dark, listening to music.
> He never mentioned it . . .

The speaker's father, who is something of a hero in this narrative, was also someone who didn't communicate with his son. In the end, the true subject of the poem is not the dramatic incident it opens with but what goes unsaid between the father and the son.

We've seen how Levis lingers on the most important parts of the poem, creating an almost cinematic vividness, and then speeds through less important scenes. Now let's look briefly at metaphor, the fastest mode of travel. Say something *is* something else, and you instantly transport the reader to that new place or thing (metaphor,

from the Greek, 'To transfer or transport'). Levis uses metaphor to
create a scene his speaker can walk around inside:

> If you can think of the mind as a place continually
> Visited, a whole city placed behind
> The eyes, & shining, I can imagine, now, its end –
> As when the lights go off, one by one,
> In a hotel at night, until at last
> All of the travelers will be asleep, or until
> Even the thin glow from the lobby is a kind
> Of sleep; & while the woman behind the desk
> Is applying more lacquer to her nails,
> You can almost believe that the elevator,
> As it ascends, must open upon starlight.

*

> I stand out on the street, & do not go in.
> That was our agreement, at my birth . . . .

The metaphor of the mind as a city where the lights are going out
one by one is crucial to the poem, not simply decorative. Discovering
this metaphor and finding the true subject of the poem happen
simultaneously.

### *En route*: Finding the song lines

Richard Hugo, in his classic creative writing text *The Triggering Town*,
suggested that a poem has two subjects, the one that 'triggers' the
poem and the one discovered as the poem unfolds.[21] Hugo says that
one way to find your poem's 'true subject' is to use words for their
sounds more than for their logic. After arguing at length that the music
of a poem is more important than the meaning, Hugo admits that it
isn't, really, but says that if you *believe* it is you may get somewhere
as a writer. We use words every day to communicate meaning, so
meaning will come through anyway; we need to concentrate on the
sounds of a poem if the writing is going to sing. Sometimes, by
abandoning ourselves to rhythms and tones, we can 'get lost' and find
what we didn't know we were looking for.

Whether one is writing in traditional forms or in free verse, this
issue of the sounds a poem makes is essential. And just as the poet may

discover his or her 'true subject' during composition, the poem may reveal what form it 'wants' to be written in. For example, you might find yourself writing a short free-verse poem with a 'turn' a little after the mid-point and realize you have a potential sonnet in your hands; you didn't plan to write a sonnet, but as the poem unfolds you realize you could bring out what's already there. Similarly, you might write a villanelle or sestina, feel pleased for a few days, then return to the poem and think how much better it could be if you took down the 'scaffolding' of the set form and made a free-verse poem. In both cases, you would be listening to what's down on the page and trying to follow, or call forth, the music there.

This is not the place to map out the different techniques of sonic pleasure available to the poet in traditional or free verse. There are book-length texts available for this (Paul Fussell's *Poetic Meter And Poetic Form* is one of my favourites), and studying the moves of free-verse and formalist masters can be an excellent way to learn.[22] Again, I'm asking you to read as a writer. Read out loud, so you can hear what the poem is doing. Imitate.

When writing a poem, it is rarely enough simply to make a careful observation or narrate a moving story. The sounds of the words need to be considered as well. Here's Charles Wright, meditating on this issue. 'Do poems have to sing? No. Do good poems have to sing? Probably. Do great poems have to sing? Absolutely.'[23]

When writing your own poems, be open to the way the sounds or rhythms may lead you to say things you didn't know you meant. There's always the danger that you're saying something you *don't* mean but have blurted out to please a rhyme: not a good idea. But rhymes or cadences can call forth the unexpected best in you as well. Getting caught up in the rhythm of a poem can lead to pleasing surprises.

The critic Walter Pater said, 'All art aspires to the condition of music.'[24] When you're writing, it may be the moments you forget that poetry *isn't* music that you'll cherish most.

## What to do when you arrive: The art of revision

Once you have followed the poem to what feels like its natural conclusion, it's often best to move on to something else for a while and later come back to the poem with a fresh mind. One way to approach revision is to ask yourself if you've said too much or perhaps too little.

Most good writing is concise. While overwriting can be part of the genius of the rough draft – say everything and you might surprise yourself, the way Bishop did in the early drafts of 'One Art' – revision is the time to tighten things up. Here's your chance to delete unnecessary words, find one precise image to replace a clutter of abstractions, and remove anything that can be taken out without a loss to the meaning or overall effect of the poem.

There is usually room for compression even in an advanced poem. In 1922, T.S. Eliot asked his friend Ezra Pound to look at his long poem 'The Waste Land'. Eliot says he received the manuscript back 'reduced to about half its size, in the form in which it appears in print'.[25]

Pound could be equally severe with his own work. One of his most famous poems began as a 30-line rough draft, after Pound was overwhelmed by an impression of the beauty of faces in the Paris metro. Later, he destroyed the draft, but after 6 months he wrote a poem half that length describing the same scene. A year later, he compressed the poem to two lines:

> 'In a Station of the Metro'
> The apparition of these faces in the crowd;
> Petals on a wet, black bough.[26]

Compression was one of the key points in Pound's programme for the short-lived, but still influential, Imagist school. In 1913, Pound told poets 'To use absolutely no word that does not contribute to the presentation' (of course, all rules are meant to be broken, and by 1917, Pound had begun *The Cantos*, a sprawling poem that eventually exceeded 800 pages).[27]

Compression is the first principle of revision. However, sometimes a poem hasn't explored its territory fully enough, and then the best way to revise is to extend the poem.

In 1994, during a talk at the Dodge Poetry Festival, Robert Hass discussed his creative process. He used as an example a new poem, which would eventually be titled 'Dragonflies, Mating'.[28] It begins with a 13-line lyric in which a speaker finds himself in the mountains and muses on the Native Americans who lived there before him. It's a tight, elegantly written poem that could have been published in most literary journals, but Hass said that when he reread it later it felt 'slight' and perhaps romanticized the Native Americans. So he wrote a second, humorous section that describes two Indians from different tribes talking about the creation of the world ('Coyote was

on the mountain/and he had to pee . . .'). This additional material
enlivens the poem and keeps it from being overly 'earnest', but – as
I recall the talk – Hass felt the poem was now too neatly balanced.
Perhaps he used the words 'thesis' and 'antithesis' and felt it needed
to move towards 'synthesis'. A third section was called into being,
in which Hass's speaker recalls the Catholic high school he once
attended. The Franciscan missionaries who founded the school had
meant well, but along with their Christian love they brought to the
New World various diseases from Europe that decimated the Native
Americans. The poem ends with the speaker recalling how he used
to practice basketball in the school's gymnasium and be mortified
when his alcoholic mother arrived to pick him up:

> I'd see her in the entryway looking for me, and I'd bounce
> the ball two or three times, study the orange rim as if it were,
> which it was, the true level of the world, the one sure thing
>
> *
>
> the power in my hands could summon. I'd bounce the ball
> once more, feel the grain of the leather in my fingertips and shoot.
> It was a perfect thing; it was almost like killing her.

Hearing Hass read that sequence, I felt again that this is 'how a poem
can happen'. As Grennan puts it, 'you have your eye on a small /
elusive detail, pursuing its music, when a terrible truth / strikes and
your heart cries out, being carried off.' Hass had meditated on 'The
people who lived here before us' (the Native Americans) and on how
the world was made (their creation stories), and suddenly an image
came to mind of his mother (one who came before him, one who
helped make him). Like the 'saintly Franciscan fathers', who 'meant
so well' but brought 'a terrible thing' with their love, the mother
intends only good when she arrives to pick up her son, with her

> bright, confident eyes,
> and slurred, though carefully pronounced words, and the appalling
>
> *
>
> impromptu sets of mismatched clothes she was given to
> when she had the dim idea of making a good impression in that state.

Hass had found his 'true subject'. 'It was a perfect thing; it was almost like killing her' is a knockout last line. What a surprise, then, when I bought his 1996 book *Sun Under Wood* and found three new sections now followed that wild epiphany! At the time Hass spoke about writing the poem, he thought he'd found the right way to end it, but apparently the poem had more to teach him.

The first two new sections meditate on mothers and roots. The final section introduces a surprising new subject, the mating dragon-flies that now give the poem its title. The speaker observes these insect lovers in the same mountains where the poem began. There's another implicit link to the earlier sections: these dragonflies, on the evolutionary ladder at least, are 'those who came before us'. Like Keats in 'Ode to a Nightingale', the poet reflects on human suffering and envies the unselfconsciousness of life in the natural world:

> I think (on what evidence?) that they are different from us.
> That they mate and are done with mating.
> They don't carry all this half-mated longing up out of childhood
> and then go looking for it everywhere.
> And so, I think, they can't wound each other the way we do . . .

But, like Keats, Hass's speaker realizes that being one with nature would prevent him from knowing all that is best about being human. Accordingly, Hass comes up with a sentence that starts in one place then makes a marvelous journey:

> They don't go through life dizzy or groggy with their hunger,
> kill with it, smear it on everything, though it is perhaps also true
> that nothing happens to them quite like what happens to us
> when the blue-backed swallow dips swiftly toward the green pond
> and the pond's green-and-blue reflected swallow marries it a moment
> in the reflected sky and the heart goes out to the end of the rope
> it has been throwing into abyss after abyss, and a singing shimmers
> from every color the morning has risen into . . .

This poem moves forward by looking back and questioning itself. Hass could have stopped after the first section, but instead he let the poem unfold, surprise by surprise, until he reached an unexpected and satisfying conclusion.

Most of writing is revision, and it's often the most enjoyable part of the journey. Once you know you have found the place you were seeking, everything begins to fall into place. Sometimes the poem just needs compression, but be open to the possibility that by extending the poem you can explore that territory more fully. What you discover may lift your poem into a new realm.

## Exercise

Try two revisions of the poem you are working on. In the first, delete everything that doesn't seem absolutely necessary. In the second, expand the poem. What does the triggering subject remind you of? When did you have similar feelings about something else? Follow that new subject, letting the connections be felt rather than explicit.

You'll be left with three poems: the first draft, the compressed version and the extended poem. Decide which version has the most promise and go on from there. Stay loose *and* attentive. And consider one final bit of advice from Robert Frost:

> A poem may be worked over once it is in being, but may not be worried into being. Its most precious quality will remain its having run itself and carried the poet with it. Read it a hundred times: it will forever keep its freshness as a metal keeps its fragrance. It can never lose its sense of a meaning that once unfolded by surprise as it went.[29]

## Notes

1. H. Melville, *Moby Dick* (New York: The Modern Library, 1992), p. 79.
2. E. Grennan, 'Detail', *Still Life with Waterfall* (Loughcrew, Ireland: The Gallery Press, 2001), p. 76.
3. E. Welty, *One Writer's Beginnings* (Cambridge: Harvard University Press, 1984), p. 15.
4. H. James, 'The Art of Fiction', *Partial Portraits* (London: Macmillan, 1888), p. 81.
5. A. Zagajewski, 'Flamenco', *Solidarity, Solitude* (New York: The Ecco Press, 1990), pp. 151–66.
6. E. Bishop's drafts for 'One Art' were obtained by the author from Vassar College. They are more easily found and very usefully discussed in E. B. Voigt's essay 'A Moment's Thought', *The Flexible Lyric* (Athens, Georgia: University of Georgia Press, 1999), pp.197–216.
7. E. M. Forster, *Aspects of the Novel* (Harmondsworth: Penguin, 1976), p. 99.
8. R. Frost, 'The Figure a Poem Makes', *Collected Poems, Prose and Plays* (New York: Library of America, 1995), pp. 866–67. Cited hereafter as R. Frost with page number.

9. F. O'Connor, *Mystery and Manners* (New York: Farrah, Straus and Giroux, 1961), p. 106.

10. R. Frost quoted by H. Breit, 'In and Out of Books', *New York Times*, 16th October 1955, p. 8.

11. R. Frost: 778.

12. T. Gallagher, *A Concert of Tenses* (Ann Arbor: University of Michigan Press, 1986), p. 75.

13. P. Picasso, *Picasso on Art: A Selection of Views*, ed. D. Ashton (New York: Da Capo Press, 1972), p. 3.

14. P. Neruda, *Memoirs*, trans. H. St. Martin (Harmondsworth: Penguin Books, 1977), p. 265.

15. R. Frost: 341–42.

16. Quoted from *The Proof*, PBS programme on A. Wile that aired on 28th October 1997. A transcript can be found at www.pbs.org/wgbh/nova/transcripts/2414proof.html.

17. C. Wright, *Halflife* (Ann Arbor: University of Michigan Press, 1988), p. 30. Cited hereafter as *Halflife* with page number.

18. M. Kundera, *Slowness*, trans. L. Asher (New York: HarperCollins, 1995).

19. H. D. Thoreau, 'Walking', *The Portable Thoreau* (New York: The Viking Press, 1977), p. 592.

20. L. Levis, 'Winter Stars', *Winter Stars* (Pittsburgh: University of Pittsburgh Press, 1985), pp. 10–11.

21. R. Hugo, *Triggering Town* (New York: W.W. Norton, 1979), p. 10.

22. P. Fussell, *Poetic Meter and Poetic Form* (New York: Random House, 1965).

23. *Halflife*: 35.

24. W. Pater quoted by R. Kimball, 'Art vs. Aestheticism: The Case of Walter Pater', *The New Criterion on Line*, http://www.newcriterion.com/archive/13/may95/pater.htm.

25. H. Carpenter, *A Serious Character: The Life of Ezra Pound* (New York: Delta, 1988), p. 406.

26. E. Pound, 'In a Station of the Metro', *The Norton Anthology of Modern and Contemporary Poetry*, vol. I, 3rd edn, ed. J. Ramazani *et al.* (New York: W.W. Norton, 2003), p. 351.

27. *Poets on Poetry*, ed. C. Norman (London: Collier-Macmillan, 1962), p. 320.

28. R. Hass, 'Dragonflies, Mating', *Sun Under Wood* (Hopewell, NJ: The Ecco Press, 1996), pp. 6–11. All quotations from this poem (cited in the text hereafter) are from this source.

29. R. Frost: 776–78.

# Part II

# Mastering Themes

# 7

# About A Life: Writing from the Self

George Green

## Facts and fiction

Fiction writers tell lies for a living. If a travel writer tells you that there is a magnificent cathedral located in the centre of Manila, then you can buy a ticket to the Philippines sure in the knowledge that it will be there when you arrive. If a fiction writer tells you the same thing then it might be true, but I'd suggest you check carefully in an encyclopaedia before booking your flight. Of course, a lot of fiction writers do go to great lengths to check their facts. The point is that there is no obligation upon a fiction writer to 'get it right' factually. There are now guided tours available in Paris that will take you to all the places mentioned in Dan Brown's *Da Vinci Code*.[1] Those locations physically exist; he has been to them, he has described them as accurately as he is able. That is something he has decided to do. He could equally well have made up a city, or described a part of Paris that does not exist. He chose to ground the setting of the book in concrete reality, as to some extent most novels do, but that was his choice, not what he had to do. To put it more accurately, fiction writers have the option of telling lies for a living.

So much for the background of the novel. Brown's Paris, O'Brien's ships, Graham Greene's Central America, Dickens's London, all of these have the grit and stink of reality, the detail that persuades the reader that they really exist. But what of the characters who populate them and the events that take place in their streets and houses? Even the most enthusiastic *Da Vinci Code* reader does not suppose that a real old man was actually murdered recently in the actual Louvre and that he left a series of cryptic messages for a real American historian to decipher in order to prevent The End Of The World. No doubt there are also plenty of middle-aged American historians who are attractive to much younger women and who have an interest in signs and conspiracy theories, but the characters in Cornwell's and Brown's books did not – do not – exist outside our imaginations. They aren't true. They are made up, imagined and written down by people who may, if they choose, lie for a living.

The point here is the perhaps self-evident one that readers do not expect a novel to be factually accurate – although they are often pleased when it is. What they quite rightly insist upon is that it should be *convincing*. I do not know if the Civil War England presented by Maria McCann in *As Meat Loves Salt* is historically accurate in every detail, but I do know that I believed her depiction of it completely.[2] I read a lot of historical novels. I have read novels which, from my own studies, I know to be historically inaccurate or at least highly contentious, and yet I have enjoyed them enormously and not held their lack of factual truth against them. Conversely I have read novels that I know to be based upon sound historical research and factually accurate and still not believed a word of them. So where does this leave us?

For a start, all that is happening here is that readers ask the same of a novel that we asked of the stories we were told when we were children. None of us ever met a dragon or a hobbit or a handsome prince on our way to school. We knew they didn't really exist, but we were happy to listen to well-told stories which convinced us that they existed for the time it took to tell us that such things were real. The storyteller's art pulls us in, makes us suspend our disbelief for a time, and for that time these imaginary things are as real as ourselves. They exist without being real. As the Roman historian Sallust puts it, 'these things never happened, but are always'.[3]

But we do always know that they are stories, and when we read part of us is always withheld, even when we are happy to submerge ourselves in the tale. Our suspension of disbelief is temporary and conditional. The further away from the realistic that the writer pushes the story, the greater the chance that the audience will rebel and the greater the need to ensure through the telling that they stay with it.

## Fiction and Life-Writing

So much for fiction; what about Life-Writing? On the surface it may seem that the two genres do not have a great deal in common. Biography and autobiography, memoir, witness and survivor literature would all appear to derive their power and their significance from their accuracy and fidelity. The writer says to the reader, 'these things are true, I know what I'm talking about, you can believe everything that I say implicitly, that's why you should read me'. The blurb on a celebrity biography will usually say something like 'Read this to find out what he's *really* like', or 'The true story that only *I* can tell'. This is true of more serious writing as well; there are numerous books about Sylvia Plath which have their selling point in the degree of closeness and therefore unique insight into Plath's life and death that the writer claims. Life-Writing like this cannot be sold by a strap-line across the front cover proclaiming 'An entirely fictitious and largely spurious attempt to guess what happened in the life of someone the author never met and knows no more about than anyone else with access to Google, which let's face it is more or less nothing'.[4] The intimate, exclusive, authentic knowledge is the point that sells.

So, what is truth for a Life-Writer? The novel by definition dispenses to a greater or lesser extent with factual truth, using it as a launch-pad for the story, whereas Life-Writing depends upon it. Or does it? Harking back to the earlier example of Sylvia Plath, if you read the books about her by Anne Stevenson,[5] Diane Wood Middlebrook[6] and David Holbrook,[7] you will be presented with three very different versions of the same person. To some extent this is understandable. People are not simple and their lives and personalities cannot easily be reduced to a single viewpoint. We deliberately present different faces to different audiences, and public figures do it more than most. It is unsurprising that different biographies of the same person can present radically different versions of the subject, and it would be wrong to suggest that one version is necessarily true and the others necessarily a lie. This is true of biography as it is of all forms of Life-Writing. Whether writing about ourselves, those we know intimately or those we learn about through research, the same inconsistencies will appear.

We search for truth in these writings, and yet our search is compromised from the start. We seek the single definitive version, yet we accept that we will read many different (and possibly 'definitive'!) viewpoints and build a composite and incomplete picture from them. Hitler was apparently a psychopathic monster and yet often showed kindness and empathy to those around him. As a military commander he was capable of both imaginative strategic leaps and colossal blunders. He called himself a Socialist and yet his power-base was predominantly wealthy industrialists; he proclaimed the Aryan physical ideal (blonde, tall, athletic) and yet the men who surrounded him in the highest positions in the Reich were a long way from it.[8] Hitler's contradictions loom huge because of his effect on the lives of many, but most of us are no less contradictory. When we write of ourselves, we know that we are not the same person all the time. We are all capable of both kindness and cruelty, energy and sloth, perceptiveness and blindness. An interesting exercise is to ask three of your friends to describe you, particularly those who know you from different arenas, for example a reader's group, the rugby club and your work, and see if you can reconcile the three descriptions as the same person. Any book claiming to give the reader 'the *real*' someone is by definition misleading. It is partial, in both senses of the word. Our perspectives and our knowledge are limited. What such a book tells us may be true in all the things it says, but if that is so then it lies in all the things it omits.

The above can be summarised as 'people are complicated and may be viewed from perspectives that conflict with one another'. I have discussed some of the thorny issues that the Life-Writer must consider as a result of this. However, it also offers opportunities. It allows the writer to present more than one story, and to make judgements, both explicit and implicit, or to refuse them and invite the reader to judge instead. It also (I think) insists that the writer rejects the simplistic view, the sort of analysis that presents a life as somehow pre-destined or a character as wholly one thing or another. Life is full of contradiction and paradox. Writing can and should reflect it. Finally, it reminds us that life is seldom pure and never simple. It may be the case that the simple answer is the most likely, but that is only true if you have a number of competing possibilities. Just because you have discovered something that looks right and fits with everything else you know doesn't make it right. Give everything you think you know a good hard thump and see if it still rings true. If in doubt, keep digging, and if not in doubt dig even harder.

### Secrets and lies 1: Helen Demidenko and Thomas Keneally

I want to look at the issue of authenticity through two stories about the Holocaust. In 1992, a book by Helen Demidenko called *The*

*Hand That Signed The Paper* was an Australian bestseller.[9] It won the Miles Franklin Award and the Australian Literary Society's Gold Medal. Reviewers agreed that this was a harrowingly perceptive personal account of living through the Holocaust and the death camps. Readers were moved, informed and uplifted, and the book gave the Holocaust debate in Australia fresh impetus. However, some survivors questioned the details of the book, and once journalists started digging, it soon became incontrovertible that the author had not been persecuted in the way that she described and that much of what she wrote had either happened to other people and were stories she had been told as a child, or were made up by her. Helen Demidenko was eventually revealed to be Helen Darville, the daughter of English immigrants. Relatives of Darville had been in Nazi camps, but she had not. The experiences she described were either imaginary or had happened to others and she had used them as if they were her own.

Compare this to Thomas Keneally's *Schindler's Ark*, which has interesting similarities.[10] While some people took issue with Keneally's presentation of Oskar Schindler's character, suggesting that Schindler's motives were more mercenary than Keneally suggests, or that there were other men equally or more deserving of the sort of recognition that Keneally's book gives to Schindler, nevertheless the tone of criticism was very different. Darville/Demidenko's defence was twofold. First, she claimed that the experiences and stories she told were substantially true in that they had happened, even if for reasons of storytelling she had related them as if they were her own and, second, she pointed out that all she had done was what any storyteller does. The issue came down to one of personal privilege, which, if true, elevates a narrative above the sort of criticism with which Keneally had to deal. However, if that privilege turns out to be unjustified then the reader feels betrayed. This sense of betrayal runs through the debate over her book. It wasn't that she had turned reality into fiction, but that she had claimed her fiction was reality.

Darville/Demidenko's defence in simplified form was that what she had written was true in essence and that the stories had mostly happened as she described them, just to other people not to her. She suggested that the fact that the book was a respectful and well-written text that had undoubtedly moved many readers deeply was a justification for whatever deception had taken place.

This is something that every Life-Writer should think about.[11]

You may seek to inspire people to reject racism through telling the story of your great-great-grandmother who was born into slavery and suffered terrible privations through it. You have to decide whether to include a particularly harrowing part of the story which in your opinion is essential to a true understanding of your book. Yet, this part of the story is the least well documented. Do you include it anyway, justifying your decision on the grounds that inspiring people against racism and slavery is worth the chance that the story may not be true, or do you leave it out just in case, knowing that you may fail in your mission? Truth isn't relative, but there is often more than one version of it.

So, what is the Life-Writer to do? How much of yourself are you going to give away? How much of what you say will be obviously your opinion, and how much reported? Will it be in the first person, whispering into the reader's ear, or will you distance yourself, gaining gravitas but losing that intimacy? You will need to choose.

### *Secrets and lies 2: The writer*

Of course, there is yet another layer of problems here. The storyteller, with the best intentions in the world and even after taking a vow to tell the truth, the whole truth and nothing but the truth, is still utterly compromised. Let's be honest. We don't much like telling the bits of our stories that show us in a bad light, so we play them down or leave them out (or we minimise the damage by making people laugh at us, in which case we emphasise the humour, which compromises the story in the same way). We are happy to tell stories that present us behaving well, but are less keen to repeat examples of good behaviour by people we don't like. In addition, we give our friends the benefit of the doubt and assume the worst of our enemies. We deliberately or carelessly misunderstand people, or only hear half what they say. We fail to see that from where they are standing their ridiculous point of view makes sense. People lie to us and we lie to ourselves. Our personal qualities, such as cowardice, greed, lust, pride, timorousness, jealousy, and even our better qualities like love and idealism combine to affect our view of events and people. So when the writer sets out to give a true and honest picture of a person or a series of events they bring a whole trolley-load of baggage with them which has influence on every word they write. Christopher Isherwood famously summed up his intentions as a writer with the words 'I am a Camera with its shutter open, quite passive, recording, not thinking.'[12] Is this possible? He might perhaps more accurately have written 'I'm going to do my best just to record what I see and hear, and while I'm doing it I'll do my darndest to keep my own stuff out of the way', though I'm the first to agree that my version is nothing like as snappy.

I have already mentioned the various biographies of Sylvia Plath. It is plain that a book written by an admirer of her poetry will differ in important respects from one written by someone who dislikes it. A biography of Margaret Thatcher written by one of her fervent followers will differ in significant measure from that written by a Marxist, although both will deal with the same person and the same events. The biases and preconceptions contained in these examples are, on the whole, fairly easy for the reader to filter out. The subject of the book and the writer may both be well known to the reader, and even if the writer is unknown they may consciously or unconsciously lay their cards on the table early on in their work. What is more difficult is when a reader knows nothing apart from the book in their hand. To give a simplistic example, if a biography of Margaret Thatcher is critical of her leadership style, is the writer, for instance, a Conservative whose ambitions she frustrated, or an opponent who she bested, or someone who approved of her policies but objects to women politicians? Or any one of a dozen other possibilities? It would perhaps be facile to expect a writer to compensate in advance for every one of the many possible preconceptions that they inevitably bring to their writing, but as writers we must at the very least consider our own position. What are we trying to do, and to what extent are we capable of doing it?

### Secrets and lies 3: The writer and the reader

It seems to me that the crucial point is the relationship between the author and the reader, the contract between them that I mentioned earlier. When the writer presents their work to the reader the manner of doing so raises certain expectations in the reader's mind. The reader knows that all these expectations are not necessarily correct, but that the ones at the core must be. Even in fiction, authors recognise that readers cannot always know what details in their story are true and what not. Novelists writing about historical events will often put in a note stating that 'certain characters have been conflated for dramatic reasons' or that liberties have been taken with the geography and timing of the events. In the Introduction to my own first novel,[13] I admit straight away that, while I have used the structure and characters of the Irish mythic cycle *The Tain* extensively, where it suited me I moved events around and made changes in order to (I hoped) improve the story.[14] My defence was that I considered it permissible to do any sort of violence to the facts of the story 'but not to its spirit' (*Hound*: 411). I stand beside Alan Gurganus, who says at the beginning of his novel 'History is my starting point'.[15] I changed characters and events entirely promiscuously, in the spirit of the Irish *seancheai*, the storyteller who, every time he performed, was heard to add to and elaborate his tales in order to make them funnier and more dramatic. When one listener remarked to another that the *seancheai* was 'a terrible liar', his friend replied 'yes, but he's a liar in search of the truth'.

The point, perhaps, is to decide where the truth lies in the story you are telling and then protect it as best you can. If an exaggeration or an omission to the story makes it better, more dramatic, faster or funnier, so long as it doesn't harm the central truth of the story, then you can do it. If your departure from the exact events compromises what you have decided is the important part of your story, then it must go.

Why is all this important? William Faulkner said that writers must be relentless and single-minded in their exploitation of their material. If it is necessary to rob your mother to produce a great book then you must do it; the 'Ode on a Grecian Urn', he wrote, 'is worth any number of old ladies'.[16] We assume by this that Faulkner is taking the advice that Keats himself gives in 'Ode on a Grecian Urn' to its most literal extreme. Keats writes that

> *Beauty is truth, truth beauty*—that is all
> Ye know on earth, and all ye need to know.[17]

How do you feel about the idea of sacrificing things for your art? It seems to me that as Life-Writers we are in a position to do damage to others and to ourselves. It would be facile to say that anything but the most innocuously dull book could be written without the risk of treading on someone's toes, but while acknowledging the need to dig and reveal we also need to be aware that we are running risks and sure that those risks are acceptable and consistent. To put it simply, we have to sleep at night. That means being clear in our own minds about what we think and, while accepting that we are fallibly human, being honest with ourselves. At the very least, if we are going to say something revealing about someone that they might well object to, at least let's be frank with ourselves. Naivety is not a defence. We need to think it through and anticipate reactions (not least our own) and then decide what we can and cannot square with ourselves.

Even those who have the option of lying for a living need to be honest about what they are doing.

## Exercises

1. Take an event from your family history and describe it successively from the different points of view of the various participants. How many contradictory viewpoints are there? How many of them do you think are valid?

2. Choose a work of Life-Writing that you enjoyed and make a list of the decisions that the writer took about what they would and would not talk about. Where there any places where you felt that something was being skimmed over, or perhaps more time was being spent on a particular episode or person than you thought the story justified? What was the writer's agenda? What is your agenda in your own writing? Will your reader be able to work it out, will you tell them if not, or will you let them sink or swim on their own? Are you happy with your position?

3. You are writing a biography of Mr X, a well-known politician and cabinet minister who is a close friend of your family. Mr X has given freely of his time to talk to you and after a number of interviews over the last few months you have come to respect and like him. The book is almost finished.

Your have also been interviewing your family about their memories of Mr X, and as a result of an unguarded comment by your mother you discover that he was involved in the seduction and subsequent abandonment of your favourite aunt, leaving her pregnant, alone and penniless, at a time when this was regarded as something rather more serious than it is nowadays. The child was adopted at birth, after Mr X refused to acknowledge paternity or responsibility for it. You are also told by another relative that Mr X stole money from your mother before abandoning your aunt, though your mother denies this.

You confide your discovery in vague and non-specific terms to a journalist friend of yours. He assures you that his tabloid paper would pay you handsomely for an exclusive on the story, but that all the names in the story would have to be made public. The journalist also says he can find out the whereabouts of the child if you give him the details you have collected.

While you are pondering your next move, Mr X contacts you by phone, breaking off your friendship in very unpleasant language and totally withdrawing his co-operation regarding the book. That night, Mr X appears on television where he announces a government campaign to, as he puts it, 'identify fathers who do not accept responsibility for their children and chase them to the ends of the earth'.

Mr X will not talk to you at all and has denied everything, threatening to sue if you mention anything to do with the story. Your mother has asked you not to use the story in your book, as she does not want her sister dragged through the papers. Your father is furious with your mother for letting the story slip, and has told you that he relies on your discretion. Your aunt has asked you not to print the story, partly for her sake as her family has no knowledge of her past, and partly for the child's, as she is just starting a new school after getting over considerable emotional problems. The adoptive parents took the child on conditions of strict anonymity and the child does not know who her father is.

Your journalist friend has offered you a substantial amount of money for the story, and another journalist from a respected political magazine has been in touch as he wants to expose Mr X as a hypocrite. Your publisher has been in touch, very excited about the gossip that is building up around your manuscript. 'If there's half the dirt in it that everyone's saying there is, we'll all make a fortune', he says, adding that you must move very fast before someone else gets there before you or an injunction arrives.

What do you do?

## Notes

1. D. Brown, *The Da Vinci Code* (London: Corgi, 2003).
2. M. McCann, *As Meat Loves Salt* (London: Flamingo Press, 2002).
3. Sallust, *Of Gods and Of the World*, *The Marriage of Cadmus and Harmony*, R. Calasso (London: Vintage, 1993).
4. There are always exceptions – see A. Wroe, *Pilate* (London: Vintage Books, 2000) for something that comes close to this. But even Wroe talks about the man – about whom we know little – in terms of the social and temporal context in which he lived, about which we know a great deal. Wroe uses the factual to render her suppositions the more convincing. On a personal note, it's a marvellous book.

5. A. Stevenson, *A Life of Sylvia Plath* (London: Mariner Books, 1998). A classic, if partial, study.
6. D. Wood Middlebrook, *Her Husband: Sylvia Plath and Ted Hughes – A Marriage* (London: Penguin, 2004). Worthwhile.
7. D. Holbrook, *Poetry and Existence* (Athlone: CIPG, 1988). For fans of psycho-lit only.
8. Goebbels was short, dark and had a club foot. Himmler was short, short-sighted and plump. Goering perhaps came closest to the ideal but only by comparison; he was always fleshy and later became obese. Hitler himself was, to be kind, physically average. None of them were exactly examples of the tall, blond, lithely muscular and perfectly proportioned Norse Gods of the Nazi iconography.
9. H. Darville, *The Hand That Signed The Paper* (London: Allen and Unwin, 1995). The book is now on Allen and Unwin's fiction list. For a brief and trenchant discussion of the issues, see R. Manne *The Culture of Forgetting* (Melbourne: Text, 1996).
10. T. Keneally, *Schindler's Ark* (London: Sceptre, 1996). (Filmed as *Schindler's List*).
11. It is possible that this defence was 'after the fact', but it is no less thought-provoking.
12. C. Isherwood, *Goodbye to Berlin* (London: Vintage, 1989).
13. G. Green, *Hound* (London: Transworld, 2003).
14. *The Tain*, trans. T. Kinsella (London: Oxford, 2004).
15. A. Gurganus, *Oldest Confederate Widow Tells All* (London: Faber and Faber, 1991).
16. This remark is attributed to W. Faulkner, although there is no written source for it.
17. J. Keats, 'Ode on a Grecian Urn', *John Keats: The Complete Poems*, ed. J. Barnard (London: Penguin, 1973), p. 344.

# 8

# People Under Pressure: Making Your Characters Choose

Jenny Newman

---

Fiction explores what it means for characters to make choices – or fail to make them; not only in classic and literary novels, but in love stories, thrillers, spy stories, detective novels and thousands of plays and films. A choice may be romantic, moral, sexual, comic or tragic. It can stand alone or lead to a bigger, more complex choice. It may be stark or subtle, hasty or deliberate, a last resort or willingly embraced at the height of the chooser's powers. It might be an individual moment of destiny, or shared by two people or a group. A choice can be shrewd or misguided, selfish or altruistic, right or wrong. Unlike a decision, which can seem straightforward and obvious, a choice involves at least one real alternative, and is likelier to have a moral dimension.

Readers gauge a character's importance by the extent to which his or her choices shape the plot. You as writer are free to let your characters dither, make the wrong choice, or flinch from making any choice at all. But if you do not at least give them the challenge, you risk making them seem unimportant, implausibly passive or unlikeably inert. Worse, if you yourself unwittingly slide past their possible crisis points, your reader may feel cheated – perhaps without knowing why – and your plot might spring a leak, or feel bleakly inhuman.

Choice can generate story, deepen your characters and sharpen their points of view. The extracts in this chapter demonstrate how to lead up to such moments, highlight and extend them, and build on the results.

## Kick-start your plot

In fiction, a seemingly simple decision in the opening pages often gives rise to a series of complex choices. For example, Jane Smiley begins her novel *A Thousand Acres* (1991) with a morally blind old man stripping himself of possessions and dividing them among his children: a fairy tale structure that Smiley, like Émile Zola in *The Earth* (1887), borrowed from *King Lear* (1606).[1] In each of these novels plot is a slow burn, giving the old men time to repent their decisions, and their children plenty of scope to reconsider – and uphold – their morally right and wrong choices. In other novels, the crucial choice has been made before the story begins, as in Joseph Conrad's *Lord Jim* (1900): the central character once committed a cowardly act, but 'redeems' himself at the end.[2]

If you prefer to start briskly, why not spring a surprise on your protagonist, as Ian McEwan does in *Enduring Love* (1998)?[3] Joe is deciding on a picnic site with his wife, Clarissa, when a shout alerts him to an escaped balloon with a terrified boy in the basket:

> Next thing, I was running towards [the balloon]. The transformation was absolute: I don't recall dropping the corkscrew, or getting to my feet, or making a decision, or hearing the caution Clarissa called after me. (1)

Though Joe's action is rushed and automatic, and therefore not morally resonant, McEwan uses it to propel him into a choice. Joe grabs a rope and, with five other men who have like him run to help, almost controls the balloon. Then McEwan makes that choice extreme: a fierce and unexpected gust of wind lifts the balloon into the air, with four of the men still hanging on to the ropes.

> Mostly, we are good when it makes sense. A good society is one that makes sense of being good. Suddenly, hanging there below the basket, we were a bad society, we were disintegrating. Suddenly the sensible choice was to look out for yourself. The child was not my child, and I was not going to die for it. [ . . . ] Being good made no sense. I let go of the rope and fell, I reckon, about twelve feet. (15)

Thanks to McEwan's expert narrative strategies, this is a powerful variant on the cliff-hanger. Because Joe, the first-person narrator, uses the past tense, the reader knows he must of course survive. But far from slackening tension, Joe's choice to let go is all the more engrossing because he has time to reflect. The reader cannot help but consider the central character's feelings.

But McEwan's technique, though brilliant, has the following pitfalls:

- Few actions taken in such extreme conditions can deliver what many readers prefer: a choice that grows out of a personality.
- Joe's narrative voice, with its hair-splitting moral distinctions about a desperate situation, might strike some readers as overly clinical.
- Such moments of group activity take careful orchestration; if you choose this scenario you (like McEwan) will probably need to follow each individual's fate, at least for a while.
- Some of your readers might find the rest of your plot an anti-climax, like that of *Enduring Love*.

In the novel's second line McEwan lets drop a mention of the 'strong, gusty wind' that will later rip the balloon away first from its single pilot and then from his helpers. On page eight he mentions the wind again – but only as a reason for changing a picnic spot.

Like McEwan, Pat Barker knows how to make her causal moments look casual. In her novel *The Eye in the Door* (1993), Billy Prior has come from a failed sexual encounter with a woman and 'happens to be' brooding on a London park bench over his need for sex when an anonymous man asks him for a light:[4]

> Automatically, Prior began tapping his pockets. At first, he hardly registered the existence of the speaker, except as an unwelcome inter-ruption to his thoughts, but then, as he produced the matches, some unconsciously registered nervousness in the other man's voice made him look up. He had been going to offer the box, but now he changed his mind, took out a match and struck it himself. (8)

As in *Enduring Love*, the hasty, half-conscious decision (producing the matchbox) soon leads to a choice (striking the match). Unlike McE-wan, Barker starts small, and this scene is far less dramatic than Joe's disrupted picnic. However, she has plotted the moment with care and, like all the best choices, Billy's seemingly commonplace gesture involves a test of nerve. Through the anxiety in the speaker's voice, Barker subtly reminds us that, in those days before the Wolfenden Act, Billy is putting himself on the line. Once the chapter is under-way, the danger is made explicit: even consenting homosexual males risked disgrace plus 2 years' imprisonment with hard labour. McEwan's 'hook' was, can the men control the tearaway balloon? Barker asks, how much will Prior risk to slake his need for sex? Will he trust the other man and advance into possible danger?

Once the balance of power between your characters starts to shift, your plot is underway. McEwan's random bunch of men lose against the non-human: a wind that drops then suddenly rises again. Barker's characters, on the other hand, jockey with each other. Aware that the anonymous man has risked a rebuff, Prior is tempted to tease him, and build on his own advantage: a forecast of the temperature-raising sadism he will consider a few pages further on. For now, however, he moves closer and asks the man if he has anywhere they can go, thus briefly relinquishing power by offering a choice in his turn.

## Exercises

1. Write about an interrupted choice – just before 'yes' or 'no' – which builds tension through deferral.

2. Describe a homosexual proposition where one character is not 'out'.

3. Write an interior monologue for someone who knows a moment of choice is coming. Let it reveal their heightened consciousness, or their doubts and hesitations.

### Sharpen and develop point-of-view

In *The Eye in the Door*, the anonymous man takes Billy Prior to his neglected but elegant home in a nearby square. Still in the early pages, we wait for Barker to tell us what her characters look like. First, she manoeuvres them into a drawing room from which neither could escape without loss of face. Then, instead of letting description slacken the pace, she makes it an aspect of each character's risk assessment, deftly swapping the viewpoint halfway through the paragraph:

> Covertly, they examined each other. Manning had a very round head, emphasized by thick, sleek dark hair which he wore brushed back with no parting. His eyes were alert. He resembled some kind of animal, Prior thought, an otter perhaps. Manning saw a thin, fair-haired man, twenty-three or four, with a blunt-nosed, high-cheekboned face and a general air of picking his way delicately through life. (9–10)

The chapter becomes a modern-day version of an awkward proposal scene, with Barker confining herself to Prior's point-of-view. Single and working-class, he sits to drink whisky with the man he has learnt from the envelopes in the hall is called Captain Manning. Everything Prior sees – the drawing-room grand piano, the photograph of Manning's wife with their two sons – heightens his outraged sense of the class divide. Though both men have tacitly expressed a willingness to have sex, note how Barker, unlike McEwan, postpones the moment of choice: 'If this went on [thought Prior] they'd demolish the whole bloody bottle and still be swopping regimental chit-chat at midnight' (11).

Prior, a working-class officer and hence only a 'temporary gentleman', divines that Manning cannot initiate sex with a social equal. So, Prior's gestures become as seductive and astute as Gwendolen Harleth's in George Eliot's *Daniel Deronda* (1876), when she first catches Grandcourt's eye at an archery contest, or of Jane Austen's Mary Crawford in *Mansfield Park* (1814), whose bare upper arms transfix the inexperienced Edmund as she strums her harp.[5]

> [Prior] took off his tie, tunic and shirt, and threw them over the back of a chair. Manning said nothing, simply watched. Prior ran his fingers through his cropped hair till it stood up in spikes, lit a cigarette, rolled it in a particular way along his bottom lip, and smiled. He'd transformed himself into the sort of working-class boy Manning would think it was all right to fuck. A sort of seminal spittoon. (11)

Aroused at last, Manning leads Prior up to the freezing little attic room of his absent maids whose uniforms are hanging in the closet:

> 'I needed that,' [Manning] said, when it was over. 'I needed a good fucking.' *You all do*, Prior thought. Manning went to the bathroom. Prior reached out and turned the looking-glass towards him. Into this glass they had looked, half past five every morning, winter and summer, yawning, bleary-eyed, checking to see their caps were on straight and their hair tucked away. He remembered his mother telling him that, in the house where she'd worked, if a maid met a member of the family in the corridor she had to stand with her face turned to the wall. (14)

When Prior buries his nose in a uniform's armpits and impulsively inhales the smell of sweat, it brings home to the reader his class-based vulnerability, underlines the emotional cost of his time with an upper-class pick-up – and adds a touch of humour when Manning returns to the room, sees Prior with a uniform held against him, and looks momentarily daunted.

## Exercises

1. Describe a moment of choice when a crucial prop breaks, fails or goes missing: for example, Manning runs out of whisky; the maid's bed collapses or Mrs Manning arrives unexpectedly with the children, hears a noise and runs upstairs.

2. Write about a choice that ends in violence, as Prior's might have done.

3. Describe a choice which shifts the balance of power. Write from the point of view of the newly disempowered, then rewrite the scene from the other character's perspective.

### Keep your characters under pressure

Barker's Prior and Manning, like McEwan's Joe, might strike you as chilly at points, and over-strategic. If you prefer your choices to be full-blooded, why not turn for your models to Victorian fiction, whose driving-force is the (often tortuous and unexpected) exposure of the link between action and outcome?

Nineteenth-century novelists wrote at a time when divorce was almost impossible. For women, in particular, a wrong or misguided choice of a marriage partner could, in extreme cases, lead not only to mental torture but also to loss of their children and destitution. As many bravura chapters indicate, marriage proposals were often women's biggest test of brains, intuition and spirit. Nor are marriage-minded plots outmoded today, as is shown by the number of readers and viewers still enthralled by Charlotte Brontë's *Jane Eyre* (1847), Jane Austen's *Pride and Prejudice* (1813) and *Sense and Sensibility* (1811) – and Helen Fielding's *Bridget Jones's Diary* (1996).[6] Heroines such as Jane Eyre, Elizabeth Bennet and Eleanor Dashwood are all above reproach – and make shrewd choices to boot. But do not be afraid to let your characters make mistakes. Misguided choices heighten the reader's sympathy, as in George Eliot's *Middlemarch* (1871–1872), when clever, idealistic Dorothea Brooke decides, to her sister's surprise, to refuse a wealthy, genial aristocrat and marry a frowsty clergyman.[7] Dorothea comes to regret her choice – and grows more likeable and compassionate than her rather priggish early self.

Even a morally reprehensible choice can deepen the reader's involvement, as in Chapter 27 of *Daniel Deronda*, which belongs to a section entitled 'Maidens Choosing'. When the rich but villainous Grandcourt proposes to Gwendolen, Eliot loads the dice both for and against his success. On the one hand, Gwendolen knows that Grandcourt is morally if not legally committed to Mrs Glasher, the mother of his children. On the other, he promises that he will make good Gwendolen's mother's recent loss of her fortune. Here is Gwendolen, with Grandcourt, and 'conscious of being at the turning of the ways' (224):

> 'You accept what will make such things a matter of course?' said Grandcourt, without any new eagerness. 'You consent to become my wife?'
>
> This time Gwendolen remained quite pale. Something made her rise from her seat in spite of herself and walk to a little distance. Then she turned and with her hands folded before her stood in silence.
>
> Grandcourt immediately rose too, resting his hat on the chair, but still keeping hold of it. The evident hesitation of this destitute girl to take his splendid offer stung him into a keenness of interest such as he had not known for years. None the less because he attributed her hesitation entirely to her knowledge about Mrs Glasher. In that attitude of preparation he said –
>
> 'Do you command me to go?' No familiar spirit could have suggested to him more effective words.
>
> 'No,' said Gwendolen. She could not let him go: that negative was a clutch. She seemed to herself to be, after all, only drifted towards the tremendous decision: – but drifting depends on something besides the currents, when the sails have been set beforehand.
>
> 'You accept my devotion?' said Grandcourt, holding his hat by his side and looking straight into her eyes, without any other movement. Their eyes meeting in that way seemed to allow any length of pause; but wait as long as she would, how could she contradict herself? What had she detained him for? He had shut out any explanation.
>
> 'Yes,' came as gravely from Gwendolen's lips as if she had been answering to her name in a court of justice. (225)

Eliot likes to sift her characters' worth, and could have subjected her readers to Gwendolen's abstract musings on the nature of her choice. Instead, she reveals her heroine's motives by putting her under pressure in this unsparing and highly moral scene. Though Gwendolen's mind felt divided during her frightening drift, her 'yes', when it finally comes, seems ineluctable because it was well prepared for ('the sails have been set'). Gwendolen's choice, as in all good scenes, results in a shift of power, even though she thinks she has the upper hand. Note how Eliot deftly swaps point of view: a risky technique but justified for showing us that Grandcourt knows that Gwendolen knows about Mrs Glasher. Note also Eliot's playful use of props: Grandcourt's hat heightens his air of suavity and menace, just as the maid's dresses in Manning's attic intensify our response to Billy Prior. Grandcourt uses this important accoutrement to underline his silkily delivered threat to leave. First (before the extract begins), his hat is in his left hand. When Gwendolen pales and rises (thus responding to his strategy), he rises too and rests the hat on the chair (but still keeps hold of it. His visit could go either way). When he asks her to accept his devotion, he holds his hat by his side (How will she respond? It's up to her). Only when she has accepted him does he lay his hat down, finally signalling his willingness to remain.

Unless you are writing pastiche or historical novels, your characters are unlikely to have live-in servants or wear hats on a summer day or talk like Grandcourt and Gwendolen. Nor would many modern heroines fail to raise the matter of a suitor's justly indignant mistress. As critic Molly Haskell points out, for most modern couples the 'distance between desire and consummation, the formal dance of approach and recoil' has disappeared.[8]

For successful modern sex or proposal scenes, Haskell recommends 'a huge dollop of gender perversity just below the surface'.[9] This is nothing new. Grandcourt is clearly a sadist; Rochester, in *Jane Eyre*, disguises himself as a woman in order to fathom Jane, and in Thomas Hardy's *Tess of the d'Urbervilles* (1891) the heroine returns to the sensual Alec, her one-time seducer.[10] Those who have learnt to decode Victorian fiction may well agree with Haskell that 'it was always the perversity, the misfitness, the complementary neuroses of the couples that drew them together over the more logical and officially approved "fitting" engagements'.[11] With their caddish behaviour and blatant sex appeal, these men are the forebears of Daniel Cleaver in *Bridget Jones's Diary*.

## Exercises

1. Write a contemporary offer of marriage which, like Grandcourt's, might be perceived as hazardous. To quote Haskell, your challenge will be to 'reintroduce the sense of danger and peril to a world shaped by the fantasies of *Sex and the City*'.[12] For example, one of your characters might be lesbian

or gay, the other heterosexual; or one might have cancer or be HIV positive? Or perhaps your characters have divergent religions, backgrounds or sexual practices?

2. The following extract shows wealthy, well-connected Fitzwilliam Darcy at a point halfway through *Pride and Prejudice*. Elizabeth Bennet, from a poor and embarrassing family, has, to his amazement, rejected his marriage proposal.

> Mr Darcy, who was leaning against the mantelpiece with his eyes fixed on her [Elizabeth's] face, seemed to catch her words with no less resentment than surprise. His complexion became pale with anger, and the disturbance of his mind was visible in every feature. He was struggling for the appearance of composure, and would not open his lips, till he believed himself to have attained it. (143)

Write a modern proposition where the comedy derives from the suitor's confidence that he would be victorious. You may, if you wish, like Austen, hint that he or she is capable of improvement and self-education.

3. Write a choice offered and decided through dialogue alone, without speech tags ('he said', 'she said').

4. Write a scene where your character fails to register or understand an important moment of choice.

## Let one bad choice lead to another

In fictional terms a choice only 'pays off' when you give your reader the chance to dwell on its outcome. The novels discussed so far explore the results of a single action. But your hero can, if you wish, make a run of bad choices – and you can milk the results. In *Love Medicine* (1984), for instance, Louise Erdrich's teenage narrator errs four times in a row, finally killing his admired grandfather.[13]

Lipsha Morrissey is the modern-day heir to his tribe's shamanic tradition. On learning of his grandfather's affair with the voluptuous Lulu, he devises, with his beloved grandmother's approval, a magic formula to cure his grandfather's infidelity. His spell requires both grandparents to eat the hearts of a pair of Canada geese (which mate for life). Lipsha goes to the lake with his grandfather's gun and sees them 'swimming here and there as big as life, looking deep into each other's little pinhole eyes' (202). Can shooting them be wise? Lipsha, in thrall to his spell, perseveres in his choice:

> I lifted Grandpa's gun to my shoulder and I aimed perfectly, and *blam!*
> *Blam!* I delivered two accurate shots. But the thing is, them shots missed.
> I couldn't hardly believe it. Whether it was that the stock had warped
> or the barrel got bent someways, I don't quite know, but anyway them
> geese flown off into the dim sky, and Lipsha Morrissey was left there in
> the rushes with evening falling and his two cold hands empty. (202)

To the reader, this outcome seems like beneficent fate, but the chilled and dispirited Lipsha stays in thrall to his spell. In a *volte-face* worthy of Gwendolen, he next convinces himself that his beliefs, though superstitious, should not be abandoned. This mental man-oeuvre allows him to take what the later, penitent Lipsha–narrator calls an 'evil shortcut': buying 'rock-hard, heavy' turkeys from the freezer in the store (203). But, like a teenage Macbeth, he finds that one bad move leads to another. Having already promised to help his grandmother, he now has to give her the hearts of 'birds that was dead and froze' (203). To facilitate his lie, he yet again reconfigures his moral landscape: the love medicine's power lies not in the hearts themselves but in people's faith in the cure.

Lipsha's boyish candour and clear concern for his tribe stop him from becoming a Gwendolen or even a Billy Prior. Linked to this idea, short-story writer Frank O'Connor claimed that 'children [ . . . ] see only one side of any question and because of their powerlessness see it with hysterical clarity'.[14] If your central character is young, you may, like Erdrich, wish to seize the chance of writing an unabashed account of his or her motives in a way that would ring false in an adult persona. Note how, for instance, Erdrich underlines Lipsha's unease by representing his thoughts strung together with commas: 'I didn't believe it, I knew it was wrong, but by then I had waded so far into my lie I was stuck there' (203). (You might also compare this moment with the extract from the thoughts of 9-year-old Sparra in *Piggy Monk Square* [2005], in 'Exercises', below).[15]

Effective choices in fiction often deepen the reader's knowledge of an epoch or a nation, a class structure, a family history, the progress of a war or beliefs in transition or conflict. In a scene made funny and poignant by Lipsha's warring ideologies, he asks the mission priest to bless the turkey hearts, now wrapped in a handkerchief. The priest refuses and so does the kindly Sister Martin whom Lipsha approaches next. Finally he dips his fingers in a cup of holy water and, in a bid to salve his troubled conscience, blesses the hearts himself. His grandmother gratefully munches what she thinks is a raw goose heart, and then arranges the other one 'smack on a piece of lettuce like in a restaurant' (206). His grandfather sits down at the table but does no more than pick at the heart:

> 'What do you want me to eat this for so bad?' he asked her uncannily.
> Now Grandma knew the jig was up. She knew that he knew she was working medicine. He put his fork down. He rolled the heart around his saucer plate.
> 'I don't want to eat this,' he said to Grandma. 'It don't look good'. (207)

For Lipsha, retribution comes straight away. At the scene's tragi-comic climax, Grandmother 'slugs' her husband between the shoulder blades to try and make him swallow. He chokes to death and – like Jane in the red-room – lapses into unconsciousness.

Outside tragedy, few characters are punished in perpetuity for wrong choices. At the close of *Enduring Love*, McEwan's Joe finally sheds the obsessive Jed Parry; and by the end of the chapter quoted above, Lipsha has relearnt his place in his grandparents' lives, in the life of the tribe and on the reservation. Even George Eliot allows her Gwendolen Harleth an early and tranquil widowhood.

Perhaps the austerest (and, some might say, the most life-like) approach to choice is to deny it to your characters altogether as, for instance, Franz Kafka does in *The Trial* (1925).[16] However, this authorial strategy can lead to a bleakness of tone which is hard for writer and reader to sustain; and which may explain why more short stories than novels hinge on lack of options. In Rose Tremain's 'My Wife is a White Russian', for example, the narrator has married a prostitute before the story begins. Now, paralysed by a stroke, he is obliged to sit mute while she disregards his feelings.[17] James Joyce's 'The Dead' (1914) ends with what he called an 'epiphany', that is, a moment of revelation: Gabriel, the central character, finds out that his wife has been loved with a far greater passion than his by the long dead Michael Fury.[18] As in many short stories, the moment comes too late to change the course of events.

When your subject is lack of choice, you might wish to sustain your reader by holding out hope to the end, as Katherine Mansfield does in 'Daughters of the Late Colonel' (1922).[19] The middle-aged, unmarried sisters Josephine and Constantia have only ever met one man who might have proposed to them. Years before the point where the story opens, he had left a note on the hot water jug outside their bedroom door in a boarding house in Eastbourne. By the time Connie found the note, the steam had faded the letters, so they never even knew to which one of them it was addressed. The narrative present demonstrates their habitual timidity through a scene in which they try to decide if they should sack Kate, their insolent young servant. Thanks to Mansfield's preparatory use of flashbacks and telling details, this striking example of a joint failure to choose is utterly plausible. It is also made bearable by its brevity, and by Mansfield's tender humour.

> 'What it comes to is, if we did' – at this [Josephine] barely breathed, glancing at the door – 'give Kate notice' – she raised her voice again – 'we could manage our own food.'
>
> 'Why not?' cried Constantia. She couldn't help smiling. The idea was so exciting. She clasped her hands. 'What should we live on, Jug?'
>
> 'Oh, eggs in various forms!' said Jug, lofty again. 'And, besides, there are all the cooked foods.'
>
> 'But I've always heard,' said Constantia, 'they are considered so very expensive.'
>
> 'Not if one buys them in moderation,' said Josephine. But she tore herself away from this fascinating bypath and dragged Constantia after her.
>
> 'What we've got to decide now, however, is whether we really do trust Kate or not.'
>
> Constantia leaned back. Her flat little laugh flew from her lips.
>
> 'Isn't it curious, Jug,' said she, 'that just on this one subject I've never been able to quite make up my mind?'. (280)

## Exercises

1. In Grace Jolliffe's *Piggy Monk Square* (2005) 9-year-old Sparra and her friend, Debbie, leave a young policeman trapped in the cellar of a bombed house with a severely fractured leg and a broken radio. Eventually he is found dead, and the police blame an old tramp. This is the passage where Sparra, who is at home, privately acknowledges her guilt:

> Me head's banging now. I didn't want anyone to find out but now I do. I know I promised Debbie [not to tell] but I don't want that old man to be killed as well. It's not fair. It was an accident. Nobody should be getting killed or sent to jail for ever. I should have told them before. Now they won't believe me, but they have to believe me. I want them to make it so I don't have to think about it any more. I want them to make everything all right again so I have to tell the truth. (190)

Rewrite the passage in the same or a different setting, demonstrating a solitary child's recognition of her guilt without allowing your reader access to her thoughts. You could, for example, communicate her sentiments through her actions, or through what she sees, or through her sensory impressions.

2. Describe a choice where the setting is crucial to the process and meaning of the choice.

3. Write a scene with a double meaning: one kind of choice is offered but is mistaken for another.

## Notes

1. J. Smiley, *A Thousand Acres* (London: Flamingo, 1992); É. Zola, *The Earth*, trans. D. Parmee (London: Penguin, 1980); W. Shakespeare, *King Lear* (1606), Act I, Sc. i.
2. J. Conrad, *Lord Jim* (Boston: Houghton Mifflin, 1958).
3. I. McEwan, *Enduring Love* (London: Vintage, 1998).
4. P. Barker, *The Eye in the Door* (London: Penguin Books, 1994).
5. G. Eliot, *Daniel Deronda* (London: Penguin Classics, 1985); J. Austen, *Mansfield Park* (London: Everyman, 1993).
6. C. Brontë, *Jane Eyre* (New York: Norton Critical Edition, 1987); J. Austen, *Pride and Prejudice* (London: Everyman, 1993); *Sense and Sensibility* (London: Penguin, 1969); H. Fielding, *Bridget Jones's Diary* (London: Picador, 1997).
7. G. Eliot, *Middlemarch* (London: Penguin Classics, 1985).
8. M. Haskell, 'A Chemistry Lesson', *The Guardian*, 31st January 2003, p. 23. Cited hereafter as 'Chemistry Lesson' with page number.
9. 'Chemistry Lesson': 23.
10. T. Hardy, *Tess of the d'Urbervilles* (London: Wordsworth Classic edn, 1994).
11. 'Chemistry Lesson': 23.
12. 'Chemistry Lesson': 23.
13. L. Erdrich, *Love Medicine* (London: Abacus, 1990).
14. F. O'Connor, *The Lonely Voice* (London: Macmillan, 1993), p. 43.
15. G. Jolliffe, *Piggy Monk Square* (Birmingham: Tindal Street Press, 2005).
16. F. Kafka, *The Trial* (London: Penguin, 1960).
17. R. Tremain, 'My Wife is a White Russian', *The Penguin Book of Modern British Short Stories*, ed. M. Bradbury (London: Penguin, 1988), pp. 382–88.
18. J. Joyce, 'The Dead', *The Essential James Joyce* (London: Grafton Books, 1988).
19. K. Mansfield, 'Daughters of the Late Colonel', *Collected Stories of Katherine Mansfield* (London: Constable, 1980), pp. 262–85.

# 9

# Writing Food

Jayne Steel

---

## The concrete and significant

From John Keats's gustatory experiments with wine and pepper to Franz Kafka's obsession with starving, for centuries creative writers have shown a fascination with food. And this fascination is imaginatively inscribed in their work in a concrete and *significant* manner. Recipe books achieve this twofold function all the time: they list the concrete, culinary details of a recipe ('3 cloves of garlic') then make these details significant (the resultant meal). Let's look at how creative writers deploy food in a similarly twofold way.

Sticking with 'garlic', we could begin a story where the main character, say, an elegant middle-aged English woman, stands glaring at a mound of fleshy pink garlic bulbs displayed on a London market stall (concrete detail). We get access to her thoughts, to recollections of childhood and her subsequent lifelong dislike of all things French; a prejudice rooted in her being route-marched around Paris every August by her fanatically snobbish parents whom she hasn't seen for 10 years but, for reasons yet to be revealed, has got to meet today (the concrete detail is now significant).

So, whether it be garlic or goat's cheese, food and lack of food, can be used in fiction *significantly*. This is why, during the course of a teaching year, I always devote a workshop to the topic of 'writing food'. Here, after reading short and relevant extracts from poetry and prose, students explore how 'writing food', and the related practices of eating and drinking (or indeed starvation), can enhance their work.

These aspects (which also form the bases of on-the-spot writing exercises) include,

- Use of the senses (touch, smell, sight, taste).
- Metaphor and symbolism (spilling red wine on a wedding dress signals a bad omen).
- Character development and conflict plus advancement and pivotal moments in the plot (a newly divorced, health conscious guy staring dismally at his bland, massively E numbered, microwave meal for 'one'; a hostess trying too hard to impress; an embarrassing *faux pas* with spaghetti on a first date in a swanky restaurant).
- The showing of location, class and culture (a Skegness shop, a Bombay spice market, a New York coffee house, a Soho bistro).

Bearing these points in mind, the following chapter is designed to stimulate, and put into practice, ideas about 'writing food'.

### More than just an image

In his poem 'The Eve of Saint Agnes', Keats shows a young man called Porphyro laying out a sumptuous feast on a bed where his true love, a virgin named Madeline, sleeps. The feast is comprised

> Of candied apple, quince, and plum, and gourd,
> With jellies soother than the creamy curd,
> And lucent syrups, tinc with cinnamon;
> Manna and dates, in argosy transferred
> From Fez; and spiced dainties, every one,
> From silken Samarkand to cedared Lebanon.[1]

This list of highly exotic and highly erotic ingredients functions at a number of levels. Clearly, senses such as taste and smell ('candied', 'creamy', 'lucent', 'spiced' and 'cedared') and touch ('silken') are summoned through the vivid description of the food. Keats definitely *shows*, rather than *tells*, the feast. But, as writers, we want our description to do more than this. As mentioned earlier, the description needs to be concrete *and* significant. Keats achieves this dual function because the exotic food he displays before our eyes provides location ('Fez', 'Samarkand', 'Lebanon') as well as a sense of the erotic (the food is like a heady drug, placed there by Porphyro to tempt, delight and seduce Madeline). All this summons questions about character and plot. Is Porphyro a gallant and romantic courtly gentleman bearing gifts?

Or does the food have a 'price-tag' anticipating sex as payment? Such questions are vital to our narratives, are what keep our readers reading. Shown not told, concrete and significant detail, the summoning of questions, Keats's culinary lexis does several things at once.

We can take note of other poets who have served up food in significant ways. In W. S. Merwin's 'Strawberries', the child narrator associates the death of his father with 'a wagon [ . . . ] of strawberries' glimpsed at the same moment as the 'wagon [carrying] his father's casket'.[2] But, in a poignant, symbolic and ironic twist at the end of the poem, the child's grief is soothed when his mother serves 'strawberries [ . . . ] for breakfast' (line 22). Her cheery, present-tense announcement, 'we have strawberries', strikes an optimistic chord, implying that future pleasures might eventually replace the grief of the present and the past (line 23).

In Edwin Morgan's poem, also titled 'Strawberries', the fruit presents an image for the narrator that prompts 'the taste of strawberries in my memory', recollections of a love affair and a precise occasion when, during a 'sultry afternoon', 'strawberries glisten[ed] in the hot sunlight'.[3] Take also Li-Young Lee's poem titled 'Persimmons' (Chinese apples) where, for the adult, male narrator, a painting of the fruit is the catalyst to a gamut of childhood memories and emotions: his schooldays when a teacher 'brought a persimmon to class'; his 'mother [who] said every persimmon has a sun inside'; his father becoming 'blind', and 'one night' when:

> I gave him the persimmons,
> swelled, heavy as sadness,
> and sweet as love.[4]

## Family and conflict

Writing the past through a character's memories is a good tactic for showing that character and their back-stories. And the poetry discussed above implies how food might activate memories at a sensory and emotional level. Food makes our characters recall occasions, conflict, relationships. A factual example of this idea can be found in *The Anthropology of Food and Body: Gender, Meaning and Power*, where Carole M. Counihan supplies a childhood memoir from an Italian woman called Elda who says,

> I remember when I was little, I entered my house and I smelled from afar the fragrance of the broth that was cooking on the stove. I loved the smell [ . . . ].[5]

Here, the 'fragrance' of 'broth' is intimately linked to family (a set of relationships) and home (a location), and the stage is set for writing emotion, occasion and conflict. Our characters might, of course, 'look back' fondly to a time and place that was secure and happy (in contrast to their current adult trials and tribulations).

Alternatively, though, memories about food, family and the home might provide a vehicle through which to show psychological traumas that survive to haunt adulthood. Elda's memoir, for example, culminates to reveal how food, family and the home was instrumental to her suffering from anorexia:

> I realized as an adult why I didn't eat [ . . . ] because in my house there was so much discord between my father and my mother. I felt so much anguish, so much fear, and I have this defect that when something bothers me, my stomach closes, and I can't eat. (184)

The subversion of idealized images of food and the home gives us the opportunity to show conflict. After all, smiling and convivial families gathered round the table for a home-cooked, hearty meal prompts a tableau (or cliché); as evidenced by numerous TV commercials. When this cliché is challenged, when we show discord, our characters are often more convincing, more 'like us'. Food can *structure* such discord, as demonstrated in Jennifer Johnston's novel, *Shadows on Our Skin*.[6] The extract I have chosen takes place during breakfast at a dysfunctional and working-class Belfast home. The point-of-view is that of a child (Joe) who is angry because his brother (Brendan) has returned home and appropriated his bed:

> 'When Brendan's away, can I go back into my own bed again?'
> Monday. That awful morning. Homework not finished. Winter sunshine trying to edge its way through net curtains. Ashes and dust still blowing through the tired streets. Mam's face full of pain at having to move into yet another week. He could hear Brendan moving upstairs and the pan sizzled for the working man.
> 'You'll stay where you are.'
> 'Ah, Mam . . .'
> 'I spoke,' she said sharply. 'I spoke and that's that [ . . . ]
> 'But that's my bed he's in. It isn't fair.'

'Will you quit. Just quit.' She spooned some fat over the egg in the
pan. He visualized the face of the egg turning from yellow to faintest
pink. 'Life isn't fair and it's time you knew it.'

He swallowed down a mouthful of tea and got up from the table.

'Finish your toast.'

She had eyes in the back of her head.

'I've had enough.'

She slammed the spoon down on the top of the stove, but said nothing.
He picked his school bag up from the floor and left the room.

[ . . . ] Brendan was in the passage [ . . . ] He went in to the kitchen to
have his pink egg and bacon crisp and curled round the edges. He would
remain untouched by Mam's anger. Joe banged the door as he went out.
(120–121)

Here, Joe's deep, sibling resentment of Brendan is heightened by the
fact that their mother has favoured Brendan in terms of the breakfast
as well as the bed. While Joe gets only toast, Brendon gets bacon and
eggs: 'a fry for the working man'. Notice too how this resentment
over the food is sharpened by the meticulous detail within Joe's
observations about 'the face of the egg turning from yellow to faintest
pink', an image repeated at the end of the scene when Brendan is
treated to 'pink egg and bacon crisp and curled around the edges'.

So, when it comes to writing food in imaginative and meaningful
ways, Johnston's novel shows how we can make this work for prose
as well as poetry.

### Desire and denial

And the same applies to a novel by Joanne Harris: *Chocolat*.[7] For
those unfamiliar with the story, here is a synopsis:

Vianne Rocher, a mysterious and beautiful stranger, arrives in the
French village of Lansqenet. She opens a chocolate shop and cafe
opposite the church. This makes the priest, Father Reynaud, furious because he thinks that Vianne will tempt his parishioners into
sin. After all, it is Lent, a time for vows of self-denial not self-
indulgence. He bitterly condemns Vianne and her chocolate merchandise, demands that his parishioners must boycott the shop and
save their souls.

In spite of Reynaud, the shop becomes a refuge for the villagers,
somewhere to confess their long-kept secrets, somewhere to express
their long-hidden fantasies. But when Vianne announces that she
will hold an Easter Chocolate Festival, Reynaud launches a religious

campaign that splits the village. A conflict rages between those who follow the so-called 'pagan' (Vianne and chocolate) and those who follow the so-called 'divine' (Reynaud and Lent).

The French location in *Chocolat* complements the highly seductive, almost Keatsian, food imagery. And, like Keats, Harris's food supplies us with a highly effective resource for the portrayal of location. Why else would travel guides bother to devote so many pages to informing their readers about local cuisine? In spite of our so-called 'multiculturalism', food still summons a specific sense of place. Jean-Robert Pine has a point when he says that:

> gastronomy [ . . . ] maintains close ties with the landscape and the social environment. There are some gustatory sensations forever inscribed in gold in the memory or giving rise to literature.[8]

In *Chocolat*, Harris 'inscribe(s)' 'gustatory sensations' to show us a picturesque location where 'smells of vanilla essence and cognac and caramelized apple and bitter chocolate' both stimulate the senses and harmonize with themes such as desire, seduction, denial, memory, loss and grief (125). She also demonstrates how our writing of themes can be effectively fused with character, conflict and plot. For instance, in the case of the priest, lurking beneath his Lenten and masochistic hungering, which he also imposes upon his parishioners, is his desire for Vianne's chocolate merchandise. This he itemizes in a feverish rant:

> [ . . . ] pralines, Venus's nipples, truffles, *mendiants*, candied fruits, hazelnut clusters, chocolate seashells, candied rose-petals, sugared violets . . . Protected from the sun by the half-blind which shields them, they gleam darkly, like sunken treasure, Aladdin's cave of sweet clichés. And in the middle she built a magnificent centrepiece. A gingerbread house, walls of chocolate-coated *pain d'epices* with the detail piped on in silver and gold icing, roof tiles of Florentines studded with crystallized fruits, strange vines of icing and chocolate growing up the walls, marzipan birds singing in chocolate trees . . . (33)

His rant reveals his orgiastic yearning for earthly pleasures, with the 'cave of sweet clichés' symbolizing what he really desires, that being, sex with Vianne. Thus, ultimately, in a frenzied loss of self-control, his ascetic resolve disintegrates. He breaks into the shop in the dead of night 'to touch her things in secret as she sleeps [then] pick up one of [the] forbidden fruits, taste its secret flesh [and] gorge on chocolates' (310, 235). Now, at the end of the novel, his first-person point-of-view reveals that he knows his gluttonous fall from grace, his seduction

> is like one of my dreams. I roll in chocolates. I imagine myself in a field of chocolates, on a beach of chocolates, basking-rooting-gorging. [ . . . ] Once begun it cannot end. This has nothing to do with hunger; I force them down, mouth bulging, hands full. (312–13)

Here, once again, we have a useful example of how food may resonate with meaning other than simple description. As he admits to himself, the priest's voracious rampage 'has nothing to do with hunger' but is, instead, a metaphoric rape of Vianne. And, of course, in real life as well as fiction, the conscious object of desire is sometimes a metaphor or symbol for the (real) unconscious object of desire. Think about this idea, then apply it to a character of your choosing. Hopefully, the unconscious desire will, like *Chocolat*, provide a catalyst to a plot.

As mentioned, in *Chocolat* food also summons the themes of memory, loss and grief. This is apparent when we see Vianne preparing an extravagant party feast for an elderly, terminally ill, yet feisty, lady she has befriended. During the preparations, Vianne's mind drifts back to poignant memories of her late mother, memories that flesh out the back-story to Vianne's life:

> We were never alike, she and I. She dreamed of floating, of astral encounters and secret essences: I poured over recipes and menus filched from restaurants where we never could afford to dine [ . . . ].
> Poor Mother. When cancer had eaten away the best of her she was vain enough to rejoice at the lost weight. And while she read her [Tarot] Cards and muttered to herself, I would leaf through my collection of cookery cards, incanting the names of never-tasted dishes like mantras, like the formulae of eternal life. *Boeuf en daube. Champignons farcis à la grècque. Escalopes à la Reine. Crème Caramel. Schokoladentorte.* (296)

Here we should note the way that Harris shows characters through their affinity with (or passion for) food. And fiction needs passion, our writing thrives upon it. As writers, we sacrifice many creative opportunities if we think about food as just a basic human need. In psychoanalytical terms, need is a physical lack that can be fulfilled (a full stomach), whereas desire is based upon a yearning, a passion, an obsession that cannot be satisfied. Once desire is fulfilled, it's no longer desire (in the words of Reynaud, Harris's guilt-ridden priest: 'deprivation gives [ . . . ] pleasure' (89)). In our stories, poems, stage plays and screen plays, desire can take many forms: a long-distance lover, an Armani jacket, a book publication or, for the French villagers within Harris's narrative, 'what's forbidden' during Lent: 'a tall glass of mocha' with 'a splash of Kailua to the froth' (82, 81).

## Fasting or feasting

Our stories can portray how food is intimately linked to desire, excess, passion and conflict, how we do not simply 'eat to live'. Our relationships with food is both physical and psychological: the mind as well as the body has cravings. For instance, take a look at the following extract from *The Diaries of Franz Kafka (1910–23)* which gives us a powerful and visceral conceptualization of this idea:

> 30 October. This craving that I almost always have, when for once I feel my stomach is healthy, to heap up in me notions of terrible deeds of daring with food. I especially satisfy this craving in front of pork butchers. If I see a sausage that is labelled as an old hard sausage; I bite into it in my imagination with all my teeth and swallow quickly, regularly, and thoughtlessly, like a machine. The despair that this act, even in the imagination, has as its immediate result, increases my haste. I shove the long slabs of rib meat unbitten into my mouth, and then pull them out again from behind, tearing through stomach and intestines. I eat dirty delicatessen stores completely empty. Cram myself with herrings, pickles, and all the bad, old, sharp foods. Bonbons are poured into me like hail from their tin boxes. I enjoy in this way not only my healthy condition but also a suffering that is without pain and passes at once.[9]

We might think of our writer's diary as the place where the first traces of a character or plot lie fallow and waiting for the imagination to 'flesh' them out. Yet Kafka's diary, with its masochistic and confessional food-fantasy, demonstrates how our diaries are (potentially) creative texts in their own right: and the ideal form through which to plumb the human psyche.

In one sense, *The Diaries of Franz Kafka* submits the author as the protagonist in his own self-analytical narrative – further evidence that the mind or psyche, and its relationship with food, is a means through which we can show character. In respect of abstinence, for instance, like the priest from *Chocolat*, a character might be, for one reason or another, someone who voluntarily hungers (the opposite being the vampire who cannot satiate enough). The many potential reasons for (as well as the many potential outcomes of) self-deprivation provide us with the springboard to make an imaginative leap into the pathological. And perhaps one of the most extreme and disturbing examples of this in terms of writing hunger exists in a short story by Kafka.

The story is called 'A Hunger Artist' and charts the life of a man who performs 'fasting' for the entertainment of the public.[10] His circus, freak-show act, his hunger, is structured in the story via 40-day intervals. After each fast, he eats in preparation for the next. But at the end of the story his novelty-factor has waned, his audience is bored and, alone in his cage, he dies of starvation. One possible interpretation (and there are several) of the main theme seeping through this bizarre narrative is highly relevant not only to this chapter's discussion about 'writing food' but also to creative writing *per se*. This theme concerns how an individual's sense of self, sense of existence, cannot be realized without the positive (or negative) acknowledgement of others. For Kafka's hunger artist, without his audience's appreciative gaze his sense of subjectivity as a human being and as a performance artist both literally and metaphorically dies. Is, then, Kafka implying that the fictions we compose are performances that need an audience, or reader, in order to remain 'alive'? Maybe, yes. Maybe, no. Either way, food supplies a highly effective theme for contemplating and *writing* this type of psychological, disturbing and ontological dilemma.

'A Hunger Artist' is by no means the sole instance of Kafka's lifelong engagement with food and hunger. As noted by Maud Ellmann, 'the theme of hunger constantly resurfaces in Kafka's texts' because of his belief that 'the creation of a work of art demands the deconstruction of the body'.[11] This idea provides a means through which we might write about food in a metaphorical or surreal way. For instance, in his short story 'Investigations of a Dog', Kafka weaves a narrative around a dog that agonizes over the meaning of life and, after many 'investigations', comes to the conclusion that the path to truth, knowledge and spirituality means 'research into food'.[12] Through 'fasting' the dog is able to communicate with other dogs that 'float in the air' (180, 163). As with much of Kafka's work, it's difficult to reach a definitive interpretation of the story vis-à-vis what the author is trying to communicate to the reader at a metaphorical level. Be that as it may, Kafka's *oeuvre* illustrates how an alternative, perhaps surreal approach to writing food can spawn some innovative themes in our writing.

In developing how we might explore a character's psyche through food, we can look at a novel by Mary Gordon, *Final Payments*, which supplies a female protagonist, Isabel, who embarks on a painful emotional journey in which her massive and excessive food consumption plays a central role.[13] But Isabel is no Bridget Jones, her binging doesn't give the reader a comical showing of a female singleton's guilt at not being able to resist 'Milk Tray', 'turkey curry' or 'Ciabatta'.[14] This is not to say that food and comedy do not make for good writing, from custard pies to banana skins, food and laughter have often gone hand-in-hand. On a more serious note, though, Maud Ellmann's psychoanalytical reading of Isabel's relationship with food is (although written for the academic market) well worth dipping into from a creative writing point-of-view.

Ellmann notes how Isabel's guilt over her father's death causes her to voluntarily serve 'penitence' by 'devot[ing] herself to [ . . . ] Margaret', a woman 'who had hoped to become [the] wife' of Isabel's father (49). Isabel's penitence involves a curious 'eating strike, stuffing herself with all the food she can devour although she is incapable of either hunger or satiety' (49). As well as reversing what we might think epitomizes an 'eating strike' (a Kafkaesque hungering), Gordon defamiliarizes expectations about relationships with food following trauma and loss. After all, isn't it usually the case that characters in stories (especially women) display self-neglect following trauma and loss? Waste away unable to eat a thing? But, ingeniously, Gordon implies that Isabel displays self-neglect through 'gluttony' (50). The following extract shows this idea through Isabel's point-of-view:

> Every day, I could see my eyes get smaller, my face become more taken up with face, with flesh. The food I ate turned into flesh, and that was what I would think about, too, as I lay on my bed – food turning into flesh, my stomach growing softer and rounder in front of my bones, my breasts getting heavier and seeming to droop from my body, the insides of my thighs growing into one another, so that they chafed and rubbed together as I walked. (Gordon: 271)

In a surprisingly similar way to 'the hunger artist', Isabel's feasting (as opposed to fasting) is presented here as a self-destructive force. Isabel's body and her sense of individuality are, quite literally, consumed by her superfluous fleshiness that is 'cannibalistic' (Ellmann: 49). Defamiliarizing our way of thinking about food and flesh, Isabel's 'eating strike' is perhaps more harrowing that the stereotypical heroine who fades away into the pale and slender waif, the Sleeping Beauty figure of popular fairytales. And this breaking of stereotype is something that we, as writers, strive to accomplish.

## Going crazy

There are numerous ways we can use food to show the psyche of a character in a story. And Bret Easton Ellis gives us another route through his novel *American Psycho*.[15] Ellis's main protagonist, Patrick Bateman, works on Wall Street. He is wealthy, good-looking, charming and smart. But he is also a psychopath. The reader doesn't discover he is insane until later in the narrative. However, when his psychopathic tendencies are finally revealed, we are forced to acknowledge that the clues were always apparent. This is a neat trick to think about when structuring our fictions.

From the beginning of the story, Bateman is shown as being manically obsessed with lifestyle, self-image and status. His doctrinaire relationship to food is no exception to this almost comic yet ultimately frightening aspect of his personality. The following passage from Bateman's point-of-view supplies us with a fabulous example of the way in which concrete and significant detail (with food) can really show character. This passage occurs very early in the narrative when we are told about Bateman's morning ritual:

> [ . . . ] I take two Advil, a multivitamin and a potassium tablet, washing them down with a large bottle of Evian water since the maid, an elderly Chinese woman, forgot to turn the dishwasher on when she left yesterday, and then I had to pour the grapefruit-lemon juice into a St. Rémy wine-glass I got from Baccarat. I check the neon clock that hangs over the refrigerator to make sure I have enough time to eat breakfast unhurriedly. Standing at the island in the kitchen I eat kiwifruit and a sliced Japanese apple-pear (they cost four dollars each at Gristede's) out of aluminium storage boxes that were designed in West Germany. I take a bran muffin, a decaffeinated herbal tea bag and a box of oat-bran cereal from one of the large glass-front cabinets [ . . . ]. I eat half of the bran muffin after it's been microwaved and lightly covered with a small helping of apple butter. A bowl of oat-bran with wheat germ and soy milk follows; another bottle of Evian water and a small cup of decaf tea after that. Next to the Panasonic bread baker and Salton Pop-Up coffee maker is the Cremina sterling silver espresso maker (which is, oddly, still warm) that I got from Hammacher Schlemmer [ . . . ] and the Sharp Model R-1810A Carousel II microwave oven with revolving turntable which I use when I heat up the other half of the bran muffin [ . . . ]. (28–29)

Bateman's breakfast ritual continues for six pages, at the end of which there is no mistaking that we are dealing with a fanatical personality. Moreover, the chapter provides a witty prelude for the terrifying events to come (in which Bateman dines on his female murder victim's offal). With Bateman, the epicurean mutates into the grotesque, his character displays contradiction through its gustatory practices. And this sort of contradiction is entirely feasible. After all, most of us have several 'sides' to our personalities, and our writing of food and character can supply the vehicle through which to convey this idea in a compelling manner.

According to Ellmann:

> food is the thesaurus of all moods and all sensations. Its disintegration in the stomach, its assimilation in the blood, its diaphoresis in the epidermis, its metempsychosis in the large intestine; its viscosity in okra, gumbo, oysters; its elasticity in jellies; its deliquescence in blancmanges; its tumescence in the throats of serpents, its slow erosion in the bellies of sharks; its odysseys through pastures, orchards, wheat fields, stockyards, supermarkets, kitchens, pig troughs, rubbish dumps, disposals; the industries of sowing, hunting, cooking, milling, processing, and canning it; the wizardry of its mutations, ballooning in bread, subsiding in soufflés; raw and cooked, solid and melting, vegetable and mineral, fish, flesh, fowl, encompassing the whole compendium of living substance: food is the symbol of the passage, the totem of sociality, the epitome of all creative and destructive labour. (112)

These, rather amazing, words are, it seems to me, a testament as to how food can nourish our creative writing in many new and surprising ways.

## Exercises

1. Make a list of nouns associated with food and eating. See how many of these nouns you can transform into verbs. Now place them in sentences in unexpected or innovative ways: 'he *shark*ed his way round the bar'; 'her ancient skin had *caramel*ized and cracked'; 'road *spaghetti*ed thirty thousand feet below'; 'sunset *peach*ed the sky'; 'the whole plan went *turkey*'.

2. Make a list of verbs associated with food and eating. See how many of these verbs can you place in a sentence to create an innovative or surprising image: 'he *gobbled* her up with his eyes'; 'it was an eye-*poaching,* head-*broiling* Cairo heat'; 'waves *crunched* the shingle'; 'she *cherried* their day'; 'he *noodled* his way through life'.

3. Taking your cue from some of the writing discussed in this chapter, show a character through their relationship to food. Remember to include themes such as memory, anticipation, desire, seduction, repulsion, temptation, restraint, grief, loss and passion.

4. Using the senses (sight, smell, taste, touch) plus concrete and significant detail, describe one of the following places from a character's point-of-view: a fish market; a butcher's; a supermarket; a high-class restaurant; a barbeque; a greasy-spoon café. Make sure the observations show us not only the place but also the character.

5. Adopting an adult point-of-view, show a childhood memory about food through one simple image (such as 'strawberries'). Develop this image to convey 'something more' about the character and their present day narrative.

6. Write a scene where the preparation of food or the serving of food punctuates the action. This action could be anything from a heated argument to a first date.

7. Think of a character and show their social class by placing them in an unfamiliar location and culture. Use images of food to portray this.

8. Write a scene showing conflict during a family meal. This could be special occasion or just a hasty breakfast. Be subtle, make the conflict escalate slowly but powerfully.

### Notes

1. J. Keats, 'The Eve of Saint Agnes', *John Keats: The Complete Poems*, ed. J. Barnard (London: Penguin, 1988), p. 320.
2. W. S. Merwin, 'Strawberries', *The Norton Anthology of Poetry*, eds. M. Ferguson, M. J. Salter, J. Stallworthy (New York: W.W. Norton, 1996), pp. 1634–35. Cited hereafter as *Norton* with page number.
3. E. Morgan, 'Strawberries' (*Norton*: 1511–1512).
4. L. Y. Lee, 'Persimmons' (*Norton*: 1878–1880).
5. C. M. Counihan, *The Anthropology of Food and Body: Gender, Meaning, and Power* (New York: Routledge, 1999), p. 164.
6. J. Johnston, *Shadows on Our Skin* (London: Review, 2002).
7. J. Harris, *Chocolat* (London: Black Swan, 2000), p. 245.

8. J. R. Pitte, *French Gastronomy: The History and Geography of a Passion* (New York: Columbia, 1991), p. 9.
9. F. Kafka, *The Diaries of Franz Kafka (1910–23)*, ed. M. Brod (London: Penguin, 1964), p. 96.
10. F. Kafka, 'A Hunger Artist', *The Complete Stories*, ed. N. N. Glatzer (New York: Stockholm, 1983).
11. M. Ellmann, *The Hunger Artists: Starving Writing and Imprisonment* (Cambridge, Massachusetts: Havard, 1993), pp. 67, 69.
12. F. Kafka, *Shorter Works: Volume I*, trans. M. Pasley (London: Martin Secker and Warburg, 1973).
13. M. Gordon, *Final Payments* (New York: Ballantine, 1978).
14. H. Fielding, *Bridget Jones Diary* (London: Picador, 1997), p. 7.
15. B. E. Ellis, *American Psycho* (London: Picador, 1991).

# 10

# Children in Fiction

## Lee Martin

---

'Never work with animals or children,' the comedian W. C. Fields once said, though word has it he secretly admired kids.[1] Maybe he was only trying to help, then, the day he slipped a dose of gin into Baby LeRoy's milk bottle when the two-and-a-half-year-old got fussy while filming the 1934 comedy, *It's a Gift*.[2] A gift indeed. Baby LeRoy passed out and couldn't be roused.

Let sleeping dogs and children lie? Not in the case of the short story where often a child *is* the gift. Children, whether young or adult (after all, we're always someone's child, aren't we, no matter how old we get?), in many cases provide the presence necessary for the most important dynamic of the short story – that crumbling of a façade to reveal, at story's end, an additional dimension of truth that without the tensions between characters and the pressures of plot would surely remain masked.

Perhaps no other interpersonal dynamic lends as much tension to a short story as that of the relationships between children and adults. When writers skillfully intersect these two worlds, characters and incidents produce a richly complex and nuanced emotional terrain. Good stories are interested in the inner lives of characters – the lives that people often keep hidden behind whatever facades they create or borrow. Never are these inner lives more likely to emerge than when characters must confront the simultaneous love and dissent common to most families.

### The precious thing hidden

Charles Baxter, in his excellent collection of essays about the craft of fiction, *Burning Down the House*, talks about the importance of

131

a story pulling 'something contradictory and concealed out of its hiding place.'[3] This, Baxter rightly claims, is how a story arrives at a dramatic and enduring truth. 'Something precious emerges,' he says. Something precious because without the mechanism of the story itself this thing would be lost (113). So often, this 'thing' is an aspect of character or situation that characters have become practiced at keeping submerged or perhaps is something they aren't even aware exists. We think we know who we are, right? We think we know the people we love. Life has a way of showing us otherwise. Such revelation is the essence of the short story.

Consider, for example, Richard Yates's story, 'Fun with a Stranger,' a story told from the perspective of a third-grade class with a very prim and severe teacher, Miss Snell.[4] She insists that her students have 'Proper Supplies' – pencils, erasers, and so on – and is mighty cranky when they don't (116): 'I don't know what's the matter with this class. I've never had a class that was so foolish and so careless and so childish about its supplies' (116). Here we see the face that Miss Snell shows her students. With evidence such as this, they believe they know exactly who she is: 'She was strict and humorless, preoccupied with rooting out the things she found intolerable' (115). She scolds her students, and they often break down and cry. They envy the other third-grade class across the hall where a younger and more friendly teacher, Miss Cleery, is charming and enthusiastic. Often, Miss Snell's students hear laughter coming from Miss Cleery's room, that sort of group laughter heard from a distance that can make those who are miserable feel even worse, marking as it does the fact that they are outside the circle of light.

Children are particularly good at certainty, and that's one reason they're valuable to the short-story writer who is always looking to turn certainty on its ear. As we know, children can be very stubborn, and when writers use them as characters in short stories they often find a way to let the pressures of the plot dissolve that mulishness so the truth of the world can rise to the surface in a way that changes not only the children involved but also our own perceptions.

At the end of Yates's story, Miss Cleery throws an afternoon Christmas party for her students at the end of the term. As Miss Snell's students linger in the hallway after lunch, they watch Miss Cleery's students go into their room. When the door opens, Miss Snell's students get a glimpse of a Christmas tree with blue lights and a table laden with trays of candy and cake. In their own classroom, it's business as usual, no signs of a holiday party in the offing at all.

Finally, Miss Snell ends the afternoon's lessons and passes out gifts to the children. All the gifts are the same; each package contains an eraser, 'the serviceable ten-cent kind, half white for pencil and half gray for ink' (125). The children are forced, now, to see Miss Snell in a different light, and it's a complicated moment when this woman they've always thought of as inhuman tries to show a softer side of her personality, but in a very awkward way, presenting gifts that can only fall into the category of 'Proper Supplies':

> Nobody knew what to do, and for what seemed a full minute the room was silent except for the dwindling rustle of tissue paper. Miss Snell stood at the head of the class, her clasped fingers writhing like dry worms at her waist, her face melted into the soft, tremulous smile of a giver. She looked completely helpless. (125)

It is a temporary moment of clarity for the children as they see that there's always been more to Miss Snell than they've assumed; there's always been this longing on her part to be like Miss Cleery, a teacher whose students adore her. She stands before her class, wringing her hands and looking helpless because she's revealed this true part of herself, the part she's kept hidden behind her strict behavior in the classroom, and the children don't know how to respond. The world has suddenly become larger for them; the contradictions a person can hold are now evident. The precious thing has emerged, and the children are too young to do much with it – one of the girls thanks Miss Snell for the gift; then the other students say thank you 'in ragged unison' and soon they're dismissed (125). They run across the playground toward their homes, leaving Miss Snell behind, not wanting to think about what's just happened in that room: 'Legs pounding, raincoats streaming, they ran with the exhilaration of escape' (125). The children can put this moment behind them for now, as children often do with moments that are too much for them, but we can't, and I dare say – if I were allowed to imagine adult lives for these students of Miss Snell – some of them won't be able to completely forget the day she gave them those erasers and then stood before them so anxious for them to love her.

## Childhood memories

Episodes such as the one at the end of 'Fun with a Stranger' are what Eve Shelnutt in her craft book *The Writing Room* calls 'radical moments.'[5] By this she means the moments that stand out in our memories, the moments that shaped our personalities. Often these are moments of great ambivalence when we find ourselves torn in two different directions at once. In my discussion of 'Fun with a Stranger,' I suggest that these are moments in which the world becomes too large – king-sized because of all the contradictions it contains, weighty with more of the truth than we could have anticipated. We all have these moments, and we can all learn to recall them. If, for example, I told you to make a list of shoes that you remember wearing when you were a child and then take one of those pairs and use it to start a piece of freewriting – if I said to start with the line, 'I was wearing them the day . . .' and then to fill in the blank with a specific memory – wouldn't it be simple to let those shoes take you back to one of your 'radical moments?' For writers, it's almost always wise to let a small detail become the lens through which we see the complicated and mysterious.

'Don't start writing about the summer your father took you to live with him and his mistress,' I recently told a student. 'Write about something smaller.'

'The mango trees,' my student said. 'My father's mistress had mango trees in her back yard, and the mangos tasted nasty.'

'Write about the mango trees,' I said. 'The rest will follow.'

So maybe we start with shoes. Here's how the 'I was wearing them the day' exercise worked for me.

When I was in grade school, I wore a pair of P.F. Flyers tennis shoes. They were white and guaranteed, at least the advertisement claimed, to make me 'run faster and jump higher.' I was wearing them the day that a classmate, David, kicked me in the shin. David was a new boy in our rural two-room school. He came from a poor family who rented a farmhouse going to ruin. I remember how he always smelled of hot cooking grease, and how the buttons were missing from his shirt cuffs, and how his nose ran and he wiped it on his sleeve. He was, as I say in my memoir, *From Our House*, 'everything none of us wanted to be' (24). I was a timid boy who lived with my timid mother and my father who often lost control of his temper and whipped me with his belt, a yardstick, or a switch cut from a persimmon tree. When I was a little over a year old, he lost both his hands in a farming accident and wore prosthetic 'hooks' the rest of his life. It took me years to understand the way his life changed irrevocably because of his accident and the rage that filled him and often spilled out onto me.

My teacher that year had instituted an Old Testament eye-for-an-eye rule in our classroom. Whatever someone did to us, we would repay in kind. So when David kicked me, my teacher brought both of us to the room where I was expected to kick him in the leg. I know it sounds horribly barbaric from our more gentle twenty-first century time, but at the time I'm recalling – the early 1960s – in that part of the world, corporal punishment was more common in our schools. David had kicked me, and I was expected to return that kick; that was the fact.

The reporting of facts, though, rarely contains the whole truth. I say this because facts involve people and people are made up of contradictions. The reporting of what happened rarely includes the more important question of what the story means to the people who stand at its center.

As I stood at the front of that classroom, I was, like a well-developed character in a short story, conflicted. I wanted to kick David because he had hurt me and because it was what my friends expected and even my teacher; I was a well-behaved child who was eager to please. At the same time, I didn't want to kick him because I felt sorry for him. I knew that, like me, he had been hurt plenty in his life. So there I was, torn in different directions, having to make a choice:

> I kicked him, but not hard. I gave him a timid kick, and he didn't even flinch. 'It's his shoes,' someone said. 'Tennis shoes. You can't hurt someone with tennis shoes.'
> The truth was I didn't want to hurt him. I knew what it was to be hurt; I knew he had learned it, too. I knew that the last thing he needed was for me to kick him. I stared into his eyes, looking for some sign that he understood I had tried to do him a kindness. For a moment, his face showed no expression. Then he laughed. He laughed and laughed, and I felt small and alone. (25)

A moment like this stays with us, becomes one of those 'radical moments' because of the contradictions and turns it contains. Our intentions often produce results we couldn't have predicted. I tried to do what my friends and my teacher expected of me, but in a way that wouldn't hurt David. When he laughed at me, I had so many simultaneously contradictory responses: I felt angry, humiliated, foolish. I intended for him to understand that I felt what it was to have his sort of life, but all he did was laugh at me and in the process, even though, of course, I didn't know it at the time, I learned something about writing stories; characters and their events are memorable when they hinge on contradiction and irony. If a character feels more than one thing at the same time, and if his or her actions produce results that are the opposite of what they intend, we're left with resonant, enduring stories. One of the first things a writer needs to feel is the emotional complexity of such 'radical moments' from his or her own childhood. Then the writer will be able to draw from that emotional memory bank when he or she invents characters and narratives for short stories.

### Turning the autobiographical into fiction

Once we've mined the emotional resonance of significant childhood moments, once we've felt in our own guts and hearts the complications and turns of those moments, we're ready to invite them into our stories.

I can still recall the day that a friend, after reading some of my stories, said to me, 'All of your characters are maimed in some way, either physically or emotionally.' She was right, and when she said what she did, I had to face that fact directly. To this day, everything I write, no matter how far removed from my own literal experience, features characters who are emotionally crippled because they're caught between their own inclinations toward compassion and cruelty. Hmm . . . wonder where that came from? It's not too hard to figure out once you know the story of my family and how I grew up under the influence of my angry father and my kind-hearted mother. Whether writing from the point of view of a Chinese woman as I did in my story, 'Bad Family'[6] or African Americans as I did in my novel *Quakertown*,[7] or a murderer as I did in my latest novel *The Bright Forever*,[8] I'm never very far from the tensions I experienced as a child and the difficulty of trying to balance my father's fire with my mother's warmth.

You see, then, how the story of David and the day he kicked me isn't just an episode that stands on its own without history or consequence but one that weaves itself into the fabric of my family life. We need to know that characters in short stories don't exist in a vacuum. They step onto the page having lived specific lives, and those lives help create what happens in a story whose dramatic incidents in turn profoundly affect the characters involved. The family, with its complicated relationships between adults and children, provide fertile ground for this process.

It's usually a mistake to write directly about your own childhood experiences, to tell things exactly the way they happened. I wouldn't, for example, try to write a short story about the day David kicked me.

I wouldn't fashion characters meant to replicate David, my teacher, and me, and then try to dramatize the events of that day. That strategy would ask me to stand too close to the material. I'd feel obligated to get onto the page everything exactly the way it happened; consequently, I wouldn't have the sort of emotional and aesthetic distance I'd need in order to be able to see clearly. I'd be immersed in the experience to the point that it would swallow me up, close off unexpected opportunities and mysteries. I'd be lost in the forest, so to speak, and all I'd be able to see would be the trees. The truth is that most of us need the perspective that invention requires so we can be open to connections that we might otherwise forego if we feel obligated to only tell the story the way we remember it happening. A better strategy is to play a trick on the heart and the mind by inventing characters and situations that come from your imagination and not your memory. Emily Dickinson said, 'Tell all the truth but tell it slant.'[9] That's what I'm suggesting we do in our stories. We tell our memories slantwise. We let real experience blend with the imagination, thereby creating a story that more powerfully expresses the emotional complexity that we've carried with us all these years.

My story of David appears in almost everything I write, but never directly. It shows itself in 'Bad Family,' the story of Miss Chang who, as the story opens, is in a dance class at a YMCA in Nebraska. The instructors happen to be her ex-husband and his new wife. Here's the opening paragraph:

> Each Wednesday, Miss Chang drives downtown to the YMCA where for two hours couples practice the waltz, the swing, the Texas Two-Step. Often, she stands at the fringe of the dancers because she comes alone and must wait until she has worked up enough nerve to say to another woman, 'You must excuse, yes?' Usually, the other women relinquish their partners to her graciously, but from time to time someone will hesitate, obviously annoyed, obviously wishing Miss Chang would choose some other couple to disturb. 'That Chinese woman,' she hears someone say one night. 'Why would a Chinese woman want to learn the Cotton-Eyed Joe?.' (38)

Though I'm far removed from Miss Chang's experiences, never having lived the history I invent for her, once you know my story about David you can see, even in this opening, how it's creeping into the characters and the narrative. You'll notice, for example, how Miss Chang contains qualities of both David and me. Like me, she's shy. Like David, she's outside the group and eager to belong. She has never been graceful, and her body is bulky. In one scene, Miss Chang finds herself dancing with her ex-husband, Don, who is trying to teach her the waltz. She expects that, as he has done with other students, he will at some point press against her hand, freeing them from the simple 1–2–3 pattern their steps make, and promenade her backward across the room. Then she'll escape her own bulky weight and feel graceful as she glides over the polished floor:

> But Don never presses against her hand. He keeps her moving in the simple 1–2–3 box, and soon she starts to feel the insult of it all. He doesn't think her capable of anything beyond tracing that box over and over, and once she knows that, she feels a great rage and shame rise up in her. (42)

Everything that Miss Chang feels in this moment comes from the contradictory emotions I felt when David laughed at me, turning my expectations upside down. Though I'm not writing about myself directly, the emotional resonance and compilation of my own experience comes into the story. I can empathize with Miss Chang. I know better what she feels because it's exactly what I felt at one time in my life. 'Madame Bovary, *c'est moi*,' Flaubert once said in response to a question about the origin of his character. So in like fashion, Miss Chang is me, as well as my mother, my father, and a boy named David and the day he kicked me in the leg. How impossible it is to separate the child's world from the adult's or our 'radical moments' from the stories and characters that we create.

## Children and point of view

A story's power often relies on the way the writer manages point of view. Percy Lubbock, in his book *The Craft of Fiction*, stresses the importance of the author deciding 'how to present the story, how to tell it in a way that will give the effect he desires...'[10] When we think about how to tell a story, we inevitably have to think about point of view. It's valuable, then, to consider the various ways writers operate with point of view in stories involving children, and what those stories teach us about *how* we see becomes *what* we see.

Sometimes a child provides the central consciousness of a story. In Richard Wilbur's 'A Game of Catch,' we experience the story through the point of view of Scho, a seventh-grade boy who wants to join two other boys, Monk and Glennie, as they throw a baseball back and forth. The story opens like this: 'Monk and Glennie were playing catch on the side lawn of the firehouse when Scho caught sight of them. They were good at it, for seventh-graders, as anyone could see right away.'[11] It would be wise for me to say a few words here about psychic distance, by which I mean how near or far the narrative voice, and hence the reader, stands in relation to the story's central consciousness. The narrative voice can stand outside any single character's consciousness as it does in the first part of the sentence that opens 'A Game of Catch' ('Monk and Glennie were playing catch on the side lawn of the firehouse . . .'). As the story opens, it's as if the camera is shooting the scene from some distance. We have what we call in film an establishing shot (two boys are playing catch) but notice how the narrative voice immediately aligns itself with a character's consciousness as it shrinks the distance between that voice and that character ('. . . when Scho caught sight of them'). The camera has moved now from that distant establishing shot to a more intimate vision of what's being seen through Scho's eyes. Now notice what Wilbur does with point of view in the next line, 'They were good at it, for seventh-graders, as anyone could see right away.' The observation that Monk and Glennie are skilled at their game of catch comes from an even closer point of view, one that gets so close to Scho that we understand that he is the one who makes the observation, 'They were good at it.' The next part of the sentence, 'for seventh-graders,' pulls the camera back slightly to the point that this conclusion comes from what we call the effaced narrator. This is the speaker, perhaps the author or at least some definite narrative presence, who stands hidden behind the character. The effaced narrator, when dealing with a third-person point of view story that involves children, makes possible the significance of actions that might remain lost to the children themselves.

The important question is why Wilbur would want to be able to sometimes close the psychic distance and at other times lengthen it. To answer the question, we have to consider the move that the story is headed toward, the final resonance it achieves and the characters involved. Only then can we see the connection between the strengths and limitations of children as characters and the point of view strategy that best makes use of what these characters are capable of contributing and what they are unable to achieve. Scho wants to join the game of catch, but he doesn't have his baseball glove with him. Glennie agrees to give him some soft grounders, but as the game continues he can't resist throwing him a fast one, which Scho misses. It's clear that Scho isn't as skilled as Glennie and Monk, and soon Glennie suggests that he and Monk play catch for five minutes and then one of them will lend Scho his glove so he can play. Scho climbs up a tree and taunts Glennie and Monk by claiming that whatever they do – catch a ball, miss one – is exactly what he wants them to do. He gains a momentary power over the boys by claiming that he controls their actions. They stop their game and sit on the grass beneath the tree. Scho continues to tease them, claiming that he's the one causing Glennie to spin his glove between his palms and Monk to pull at his nose. Finally, an angry Monk climbs up the tree, and Scho falls to the ground. Glennie and Monk are worried about him; Wilbur describes how helpless they are as they wait for Scho to get his breath back.

When they're convinced that he's going to be all right, they walk away, while Scho, 'still bent over a little for lack of breath, croaked after them in triumph and misery, "I want you to do whatever you're going to do for the whole rest of your life!"' (1461). Notice how Wilbur uses the effaced narrator to direct the emotional complexity of this final moment by having that narrator stand outside Scho's consciousness to make clear the contradictions of 'triumph' and 'misery.' Never do we more urgently want to belong than when we are children, and such is the case with Scho. Often, though, particularly in this case of seventh-graders who would be 12 or 13, we can articulate the mix of emotions that we feel. So in Wilbur's story, the emotional volatility of children provides the means from which the end of the story grows. Consider, again, the opening of the story and how it contains Scho's desire to belong and also the chance that he won't be as good as his two friends and therefore won't fit in. In the child's world, things are so often unstable and therefore rich with potential tensions, contradictions, and complexities.

We see this same volatility at work in John Updike's 'A & P,' a story told from the first-person point of view of the grocery store clerk, Sammy: 'In walks these three girls in nothing but bathing suits.'[12] So begins the story, which is set in a small New England village. Though the time period is never specified, we know that the story was included in Updike's collection *Pigeon Feathers and Other Stories*, published in 1962. It's clear that the time period and the setting are such that these three girls walking into the grocery store in their bathing suits is considered shameful. The store manager scolds them and tells them, 'We want you decently dressed when you come in here' (1283). Sammy, as the girls are leaving, accuses the manager of deliberately embarrassing them, and then he announces that he's quitting. He takes off his apron and bowtie and marches out into the parking lot. He looks around for the girls, but they're gone and his gesture of support goes unrecognized. He turns back to the store and sees the manager in his place at the checkout. Sammy is 19 and, unlike the younger boys in Wilbur's story, capable of appreciating and articulating the significance of his own actions. In the last line of the story, as he watches business going on inside the store, he tells us, '. . . my stomach kind of fell as I felt how hard the world was going to be to me hereafter' (1284).

Because young people often act without fully considering the consequences, they make interesting characters in short stories. I don't intend to insult my young readers, but I can recall, even at age 19, doing plenty of foolish things. The point is characters like Sammy, on the verge of manhood, ready to assert himself but not fully in control of discretion, are sometimes more interesting than older, more rational characters precisely because these younger characters are less predictable. In the case of Updike's story, the first-person narrator Sammy is young enough to be rash and old enough to understand the enduring consequences of his decision to walk away from his job, learning in the process that bravado doesn't necessarily catch people's attention and the world remains indifferent to our most well-intended courage.

Short-story writers often deepen a young person's understanding by constructing a first-person story from the point of view of an adult looking back on his or her younger self. Such is the case in Patricia Henley's 'The Secret of Cartwheels,' a story in which the grown woman, Roxanne, recalls the time in her life when, at the age of 13, she came home from school to learn that her alcoholic mother had been admitted to the hospital and that Roxanne and her siblings are to be put in various foster homes.[13] Henley blends the perspectives of the adult and the child to give the experience that's being narrated a weight that it couldn't have if it were told only from the child's point of view. Here's one passage where Henley moves back and forth between the adult's and the child's point of view:

> Inside, everything was in its place, but our mother was gone, which made the house seem cold and empty. Four-year-old Suzanne stood on the heat register, her grubby chenille blanket a cape around her shoulders. Her hair had been recently brushed, and she wore plastic barrettes, a duck on one side, a bow on the other. When I remember those years at home, this is one of the things I focus on, how nothing ever matched, not sheets, not barrettes, not cups and saucers, not socks. And sometimes I think the sad and petty effort to have matching things has been one

of the chief concerns of my adult life. Aunt Opal perched uneasily on a ladder-back chair with the baby, Laura Jean, on her lap. (2)

The passage begins with the consciousness of the child who experiences, as we do, the cold and empty house, Suzanne standing on the heat register with the chenille blanket around her shoulders, her just-brushed hair held with barrettes that don't match. Then, Henley shifts to the consciousness of the adult narrator. 'When I remember,' she says, and the register of the narrative voice changes from that of a participant in the scene to that of a spectator looking back on that evening in that house with a perspective that's able to make something of those mismatched barrettes. They signify, connecting causally with the adult narrator's preoccupation with having matching things, an obsession that she calls 'sad and petty.' This single moment, then, when she sees Suzanne with the mismatched barrettes becomes something more than it was at the time. It becomes the source of the adult's behavior. That detail of the barrettes resonates on into the future, and only by shifting from the child's perspective to the adult's can Henley give the detail all the weight and significance that it holds. Then she gracefully moves us back into the scene withthe line, 'Aunt Opal perched uneasily on a ladder-back chair with the baby, Laura Jean, on her lap.' Henley is working here in much the same way as Wilbur used the effaced narrator in 'A Game of Catch,' only now the adult steps into that role as she looks back on the girl she was. The result is an added emotional resonance through the combination of the child's raw experience and the adult's thoughtful reflection on that experience.

Conjuring up the ordinary details that evoke and imply emotional complexity is the work of the short-story writer. Through the art of compression and the skillful management of point of view, the writer creates a world and its people in a way that causes a light to shine on what it is to be a human being on this earth. The scrim falls away, and we see the extraordinary in the ordinary. It's as if a luminescence rises from such seemingly insignificant items as erasers, baseball gloves, grocery stores, and hair barrettes, and then we see, at least for a time, more clearly than we did prior to the story. Children have a knack for involving themselves with such luminous moments. They are more open to the world for the world is newer to them; consequently, they feel more deeply. What they feel becomes the story. As I've already said, *how* writers choose to see, in other words, through what sort of point of view, becomes *what* they (and the readers) see. Character, theme, and point of view are inextricable.

Flannery O'Connor once said, 'Anybody who has survived his childhood has enough information about life to last him the rest of his days.'[14] So what are you waiting for? Get busy. Find those radical moments from your childhood – feel them in your heart and gut and let your characters feel them, too.

## Exercises

1. Do the shoe exercise. Recall pairs of shoes that you remember wearing as a child. Don't limit yourself to the ones you remember from a few years ago. Go back to some of your earliest shoes so you can find your earliest memories. Choose a pair of shoes and begin a freewrite with the line, 'I was wearing them the day . . .' You take it from there. Just fill in the blank. Just start telling a story of something that happened. Keep your pen moving or your fingers typing. If you get stuck, just say, 'I'm supposed to be writing about these shoes and what happened one day when I was wearing them, but I can't really remember anything. What I remember instead is . . .' You get the idea. Just get a memory onto the page. At some point during the freewrite, when you're immersed in narrative, be aware of a 'radical moment' – a moment of contradiction when you felt opposing things at the same time. Perhaps, hate and love. Perhaps, pride and shame. Find a moment and an emotional response that make you curious, that require a story to figure out how that moment came to be and what it might mean.

2. Create two characters by asking a series of questions about each of them. Here are a few examples:

   - What's this character's favorite music? Be as specific as you can.
   - What's hanging in this character's closet that he can't bring himself to get rid of even though he never wears it?
   - What's the one thing this character hid in a drawer and then forgot?
   - When's the last time this character wrote a letter or an e-mail? To whom? For what purpose? Did she get a response? From whom? What did it say?
   - When's the last time this character cried? What were the circumstances?

- What's the one thing this character would like to tell someone else but can't?
- What's this character's favorite season of the year? Why? What does he do during that time?
- What's this character's greatest fear?
- Where did this character go on his last vacation? What did he do there that he wouldn't want anyone to know?

You can use any question that helps you know the characters. Now here's the opening of Tobias Wolff's story, 'An Episode in the Life of Professor Brooke':

> Professor Brooke had no real quarrel with anyone in his department, but there was a Yeats scholar named Riley whom he could not bring himself to like. Riley was flashy, so flashy that even his bright red hair seemed an affectation, and it was said that he'd had affairs with some of his students. Brooke did not as a rule give credit to these rumors, but in Riley's case he was willing to make an exception. He had once seen a very pretty girl leaving Riley's office in tears. Students did at times cry over bad grades, but this girl's misery was something else. It looked more like a broken heart than a C –.
>
> They belonged to the same parish, and Brooke, who liked to sit in the back of the church, often saw Riley at Mass with his wife and their four red-haired children. Seeing the children and their father together, like a row of burning candles, always made Brooke feel more kindly toward Riley. Then Riley would turn to his wife or look around, and the handlebars of his unnecessarily large moustache would come into view, and Brooke would dislike him again.[15]

Using the two characters you created, write an imitation of Wolff's opening. Think about the conflicts and the potential drama that the opening suggests. Where might your story be headed? Toward what moment of emotional complexity that is similar to what you felt when you did the freewrite about your own radical event?

3. Make a list of ordinary items such as hair barrettes and erasers that you recall from your childhood. Choose one and write about it in a scene, noticing only what you would have noticed as a child. Then find, as Patricia Henley does in 'The

Secret of Cartwheels,' a place to shift to the perspective of the person you are now. Write about that item from the adult's point of view, making something more of it than you could have known when you were younger. Let the item suggest a family tension or conflict that requires a story to resolve.

**Notes**

1. E. Stephan, 'Biography for W.C. Fields,' 1990–2005, <http://www.imdb.com/name/nm0001211/bio> 24 July 2005.
2. C. Bogle and J. P. McEvoy. Dir. N. Z. McLeod. *It's a Gift*. Paramount Pictures. 1934.
3. C. Baxter, *Burning Down the House* (Saint Paul, Minnesota: Graywolf Press, 1997), p. 38.
4. R. Yates, *Eleven Kinds of Loneliness* (New York: Delta/Seymour Lawrence, 1982), p. 116.
5. E. Shelnutt, *The Writing Room* (Atlanta, Georgia: Longstreet Press, 1989), p. 6.
6. L. Martin, 'Bad Family,' *The Nebraska Review*, 25, no. 2 (1997), pp. 38–55.
7. L. Martin, *Quakertown* (New York: Dutton, 2001).
8. L. Martin, *The Bright Forever* (New York: Shaye Areheart, 2005).
9. E. Dickinson, 'Tell all the truth but tell it slant,' *Selected Poetry of Emily Dickinson* (New York: Doubleday/The New York Public Library Collector's Edition, 1997), p. 223.
10. P. Lubbock, *The Craft of Fiction* (New York: Viking, 1957), p. 62.
11. R. Wilbur, 'A Game of Catch,' *The Norton Anthology of Short Fiction*, 2nd edn, ed. R. V. Cassill (New York: W.W. Norton, 1981), p. 1458.
12. J. Updike, 'A & P,' *The Story and Its Writer*, 4th edn, ed. A. Charters (Boston: Bedford Books of St Martin's Press, 1995), p. 1280.
13. P. Henley, *The Secret of Cartwheels* (St. Paul, Minnesota: Graywolf Press, 1992), pp. 1–18.
14. F. O'Connor, 'Mystery and Manners,' *Mystery and Manners*, eds. S. and R. Fitzgerald (New York: Farrar, Straus & Giroux, 1969), p. 84.
15. T. Wolff, *The Garden of the North American Martyrs* (New York: Ecco Press, 1981), p. 27.

# 11

# Writing Home: How to Use Houses in Fiction

Jenny Newman

In everyday life, home-dwellers can misunderstand or wrongly mistrust those with no fixed address; perhaps because the homeless cannot easily be 'placed'. Likewise in novels and short stories, if you fail to give your characters 'a local habitation', you may leave your readers suspicious or confused.[1] Cold Comfort Farm, Bleak House, Jalna, Manderley, The House on Mango Street: these are more than mere backdrops. The home you create in your fiction can be, like them, both character and stage, fuelling conflict, thwarting desire or triggering crisis points, while building a sense of your characters' private lives.

This chapter looks at how a range of fiction writers past and present exploit the idea of domestic space. Six contrasting extracts about three different kinds of rooms will demonstrate how to build characters through the environments you create for them, how to describe those surroundings without slackening pace, how rooms can generate plot and how to choose the most effective viewpoint.

## Exercises

1. In his story 'Metamorphosis' (1915), Franz Kafka's description of the Samsa flat is so exact and consistent that Vladimir Nabokov was able to draw its ground plan for his students.[2] Why not begin by designing your fictional house? Is it shabby or well-appointed? Old, architect-designed, a terraced house

or part of an estate? Who chose it and why? What does the décor reveal about its occupants? What do the uses to which your characters put their rooms say about the epoch in which they live (few people now have rumpus rooms, butler's pantries, billiard rooms, night nurseries, withdrawing rooms or conversation pits. No Victorians had television rooms, work stations or jacuzzis)? Which rooms are most used and which hardly at all? Who among your characters feels most at home in which room? Are any rooms forbidden to certain household members?

2. Your readers need to be shown what your characters see as important. For instance, television sets are central to the MTV generation of Bret Easton Ellis's *American Psycho* (1991).[3] Alternatively, in the title story of *The Secret Goldfish* (2004), David Means uses the changing state of a fish tank to chart a marital breakdown.[4] What do your 'props' reveal?

## Kitchens

The kitchen is the heart of a home, its source of warmth and nourishment. It is also the site of most domestic murders and accidental deaths. This place of potential extremes is a promising room from which to launch your plot, following, for instance, Emily Brontë in *Wuthering Heights* (1847).[5] Her novel starts (like many) with the arrival of a stranger. The callow and imperceptive Lockwood appears at an isolated Yorkshire farmhouse where his host, the misanthropic Heathcliff, flouts the age-old custom of offering hospitality.

Brontë designs her kitchen like a stage set, carefully positioning entrances, exits and props. First comes the outside door through which Lockwood barges unasked. He finds himself in a room with a fireplace, flagstones, oak dresser, silver tankards, pewter dishes and a liver-coloured pointer bitch and pups. To a modern reader this might seem a Conran-style idyll; except that each detail detracts from our sense of security and heightens the drama of this topsy-turvy world. Adjectives are all the more effective for being sparing. The 'huge' fire-place, 'vast' dresser and 'immense' pewter dishes all suggest that their users are Titans, while the 'villainous' guns and horse-pistols hint at forthcoming conflict and cruelty (14). Lest we be cheered by the single glimpse of colour – three 'gaudily-painted canisters' on the chimney ledge – we soon learn it was planted only to underline a refusal to offer Lockwood tea (14). Even the dog – normally a symbol of domesticity – sneaks 'wolfishly' to the back of the visitor's legs (15).

Note how quickly Brontë has moved her characters from the less constraining outdoors, and how she uses the confines of her room to keep them trapped in unwelcome proximity, spotlight their social embarrassment then let one of them reveal himself or herself during a moment's privacy: all good methods of generating tension. A second door leads to the cellar from which Joseph, the servant, refuses to be summoned. Through this authorial ploy Brontë not only forecasts his surliness but also manoeuvres the host offstage: Heathcliff himself is obliged to dive down the steps for wine. By pulling faces at the dogs in his absence, Lockwood proves his pettiness. When the dogs attack him the third door opens to admit a 'lusty dame' flourishing a frying-pan (16). Heathcliff returns and, as home-owner, feels entitled to intimidate Lockwood. Brontë makes clear the latter's misgivings by having him choose a seat far from his host. Such adroitly timed manoeuvres do not only entertain. They also put the characters under pressure and lay bare the household's crumbling power structures.

Rooms are often 'gendered', especially in large or traditional homes where space is not at a premium. Men dominate libraries, studies, gun-rooms, billiard and smoking rooms. Women occupy boudoirs, laundries and drawing-rooms. With their saucepans, kettles, cookers or stoves, kitchens in particular are seen as a female terrain, household alembics where women connive or fight for supremacy. You can, if you wish, subvert this segregation. Brontë, for instance, 'regenders' the site of her opening conflict by banishing utensils and the chatter of female voices to an unseen room. Her kitchen – at least in this chapter – thus becomes a space where men talk and drink wine (for another approach to masculine kitchens, see the first Exercise, below).

Toni Morrison's *Love* (2003) also begins with an intruder in a kitchen: Junior, a waif, has answered an advertisement for a companion secretary, and is confronting Christine, the maid.[6] In the extract that follows, both women sit at the table while Christine deveins shrimps.

Twelve rings, two on three fingers of each hand, snatched light from the ceiling fixture and seemed to elevate her task from drudgery to sorcery. [ . . . ]

Jacket leather purred as Junior Viviane shrugged her shoulders and reached across the table to the colander. [ . . . ] 'Can I help you with that, ma'am?' she asked. 'I'm a pretty fair cook.'

'Don't.' The woman held up a staying hand. 'Needs a certain rhythm.'

A bouquet of steam wandered away from water lifting to a boil on the stove. Behind the table was a wall of cupboards, their surfaces as pale and handled as yeast dough. The silence stretching between the two tightened. Junior Viviane fidgeted, her jacket creaking over the tick of shrimp shells. (20–21)

In Brontë's kitchen, chairs 'lurk' in the shade and dogs 'haunt' the recesses. Morrison too brings her sorcerer's lair to life by her use of sinewy verbs, like Brontë's unweakened by adverbs. The steam 'wanders' away from the water that 'lifts' to the boil. The shrimp cells 'tick'. Christine's rings 'snatch' light from the ceiling fixture.

Learn from Brontë and Morrison to identify your characters' source of power. Heathcliff's derived from his aura of masculine violence. Christine's comes from culinary magic, made to seem all the more dangerously strategic through Morrison's choice of the third-person objective point of view, giving us access to neither character's head. Christine gains ascendancy over Junior even more efficiently than Heathcliff did over Lockwood. Junior's leather jacket may creak and purr, but for now all the girl herself can do is laugh, fidget and shrug her shoulders.

All houses in fiction are haunted to the extent that their pasts affect the present. To bring your novel's back-story to life, why not try creating a modern-day ghost? The more physical you can make it, the more it will convince, as in *Wuthering Heights* where the ghost appears at the window on Lockwood's second visit. Unable to shake its grip, he 'pulled its wrist on to the broken pane, and rubbed it to and fro till the blood ran down and soaked the bed-clothes' (30). In *Love*, Morrison contents herself with 'police-heads': 'dirty things with big hats that shoot up out of the ocean' (5). In *Beloved* (1987), however (which also opens with a kitchen scene), the entire house is 'spiteful. Full of a baby's venom' (3).[7] Enter the murdered daughter that shatters a mirror, imprints her hands on a cake, overturns kettlefuls of hot chickpeas on to the floor and scatters crumbled soda crackers. Beloved is prey to the same motivation that animates Heathcliff and Christine: desire for revenge.

## Kitchen exercises

1. Write a scene where two men fight for access to a stove. Make them both excellent cooks but of different backgrounds and ages.

2. In Michèle Roberts' short story, 'The Bishop's Lunch', Sister Josephine of the Holy Face imagines a curious being:[8]

> The angel of the resurrection has very long wings. Their tips end in single quills. The angel of the resurrection has three pairs of wings that swaddle him in black shawls then unwrap when he

needs them, nervous and strong. The angel of the resurrection flies in the darkness. He is invisible and black. His feathers are soft as black fur. (83)

Her vision inspires her to make for the Bishop's lunch:

the figure of an angel sculpted from choux buns stuck together with caramel and then coated with dark bitter-chocolate cream. His arms were held out wide, and his three pairs of black wings extended behind him. A very noble confection, said the nuns: truly, a miracle. (89)

What is your hero's or heroine's most unusual recipe? For whom would they dream it up and in what sort of kitchen? What would happen to the person who ate it? Give your imagination free rein.

## Bedrooms

To some novelists a bedroom scene might still mean writing sex, but most are more inventive – or more perverse. Graham Greene's Bendrix and Sarah in *The End of the Affair* (1951) have sex on the living-room parquet when Sarah's husband is upstairs in bed. Cecilia and Robbie in *Atonement* (2001) by Ian McEwan make love standing up in the library. Michael Ondaatje's Gianetta and Caravaggio in *In the Skin of the Lion* (1988) have sex as they move from the stairs through the hall and into the kitchen. In Aldous Huxley's *Point Counter Point* (1928) Burlap and Beatrice make love in the bath. Many hardy English characters seem more aroused by the weather than by the thought of a bed, and prefer their sex out of doors; like, famously, D. H. Lawrence's Paul and Miriam in *Sons and Lovers* (1913) and Constance and Mellors in *Lady Chatterley's Lover* (1928).

If you decide to write about sex in a bed, remember it can swerve quickly and inadvertently into bedroom farce, as in E. M. Forster's *Maurice* (1971) when the hero hears his lover climbing up to his window.[9] '[Maurice] seemed to crackle and burn and saw the ladder's top quivering against the moonlit air' (167). Perhaps because sex between sheets can take careful planning, novelists often use bedroom scenes to convey coldness or trickery, as with William Golding's Sammy Mountjoy in *Free Fall* (1959); or in D. B. C. Pierre's *Vernon*

*God Little* (2003), where it later transpires that Taylor Figueroa was seducing the narrator on behalf of the police:[10]

> Suddenly her pout turns to rubber, her breeze to raw shrimp and metal-butter. Something ain't right. She scoots to the edge of the bed. Her cleft sneers through the silk of her panties as she bends over one last time. I know I've had the last of Taylor Figueroa. (195)

Taylor is little more than a plot device. But novelists tend to link the beds of their major characters less with sex than with sleep and dreams. Charlotte Brontë's fictional bedrooms, for instance, are usually sites of psychical transformations; other-worldly spaces which propel their inhabitants into heightened or prophetic states of mind.

Like *Wuthering Heights* and *Love, Jane Eyre* (1847) begins with a conflict.[11] Sallow, flabby, 14-year-old John Reed bullies Jane, the 10-year-old orphan who lodges on sufferance in his mother's home. When Jane defends herself against his blows she is reported to Mrs Reed, who has her locked in a little-used bedroom. Note how Brontë signals the red-room's importance by describing it far more fully than any other room in the novel:

> A bed supported on massive pillars of mahogany, hung with curtains of deep red damask, stood like a tabernacle in the centre; the two large windows, with their blinds always drawn down, were half shrouded in festoons and falls of similar drapery [ . . . ] Out of these deep surrounding shades rose high, and glared white, the piled-up mattresses and pillows of the bed, spread with a snowy Marseilles counterpane. (10–11)

Brontë piles detail upon detail in her account of this single item of furniture which, like most Victorian household beds, had once been a deathbed and bier. Next she introduces one of fiction's most helpful domestic props: a looking-glass. First, she uses it to reflect the bed's 'vacant majesty', thus helping the reader to visualize one of its principal meanings. Next, she has her heroine rise and inspect her reflection: a common enough device for letting the reader 'see' a first-person narrator. But mirrors can do more than reflect the present. Like beds, they are linked with birth, though not of the body. The vision Jane sees in the glass foreshadows her future identity: steadfast, spirited, odd:

> All looked colder and darker in that visionary hollow than in reality: and the strange little figure there gazing at me, with a white face and

arms specking the gloom, and glittering eyes of fear moving where all else was still, had the effect of a real spirit: I thought it like one of the tiny phantoms, half fairy, half imp, Bessie's evening stories represented as coming out of lone, ferny dells in moors, and appearing before the eyes of belated travellers. (11)

As well as building our sense of her heroine's character, Brontë is also plotting a powerful love story. Learn from her how to write a pivotal scene, like the one described above, then return to it when you want to develop your novel's principal themes. Some years later, the adult Jane meets Rochester. In order to signal her affinity with her suitor-to-be, Brontë has the first sound of his horse's hoof beats in a lane plunge her into the past of Bessie's tales: Jane thinks of a North-of-England spirit called a gytrash. When Rochester later summons her to the drawing-room, he intimates his kinship despite his gruff behaviour by recognizing her 'mirror-self' at once: 'When you came on me in Hay Lane last night, I thought unaccountably of fairy tales, and had half a mind to demand whether you had bewitched my horse' (107).

At the end of the episode in the red-room, Jane lapses into unconsciousness: a device Brontë learnt from the Gothic, a genre which also uses bedrooms for scenes of terror and recognition. Later in the novel, Brontë develops Jane's parity with Rochester by two parallel scenes. In the first (Chapter 15), it is his turn to succumb to oblivion: Bertha Rochester has set his bed on fire. Ten chapters later Jane is at risk again when Bertha enters her room and rips her wedding-veil. Read these three episodes in succession and see how Brontë uses these different but parallel nights to reveal her characters' unconscious minds, to let them (plausibly) break daytime taboos and to express feelings they would normally keep hidden, sometimes even from themselves.

The words 'I love you' can only sound like a cliché: better to show your characters in action, like F. Scott Fitzgerald in *The Great Gatsby* (1925).[12] The novel describes Jay Gatsby's passion for Daisy Buchanan who is married to Tom. In order to win her, Gatsby has amassed a fortune and bought a mansion next to the house of her cousin, Nick Carraway, the narrator. At last, Gatsby meets Daisy and shows her and Nick round his huge, ostentatious home. The tour ends in the simplest yet most revealing place: his bedroom where, instead of the ghostly bed and looking-glass of *Jane Eyre*, we see two 'hulking' cabinets, both of which he opens (98–99). Fitzgerald's adjectives and similes deftly suggest that Gatsby's passion for Daisy – unlike that of Jane and Rochester for each other – will always be coloured by material goods. Inside the wardrobes, his suits are 'massed' and his shirts 'piled like bricks' (99). But clothes, like mirrors, in a skilful writer's hands, are not made purely for show.

> He [Gatsby] took out a pile of shirts and began throwing them, one by one, before us, shirts of sheer linen and thick silk and fine flannel, which lost their folds as they fell and covered the table in many coloured disarray. While we admired he brought more and the soft rich heap mounted higher – shirts with stripes and scrolls and plaids in coral and apple-green and lavender and faint orange, with monograms of indian blue. Suddenly, with a strained sound, Daisy bent her head into the shirts and began to cry stormily.
>
> 'They're such beautiful shirts,' she sobbed, her voice muffled in the thick folds. 'It makes me sad because I've never seen such – such beautiful shirts before'. (99)

This scene is not about clothes as they are worn in the street, but about how they can transform an intimate situation. Though Gatsby's shirts have been chosen by 'a man in England', their tumbling textures and colours reveal the passion, hope and imagination that the bemused but joyful millionaire could never express in words (99).

Daisy sobs into the shirts and not on Gatsby's shoulder: her outburst seems to be prompted by his worldly goods. Yet her expression of sadness deepens reader sympathy, and its hint of her appreciation of her would-be lover makes his passion more poignant and explicable.

## Bedroom exercises

1. Describe burgling a bedroom from the burglar's point of view, in the first or third person. How do you feel? What motivates you? Is it night or day? How do you reach the bedroom? What is it like? Are you male or female? What are you looking for? Are the owners in bed? Are you in dire need, or an antiques thief or a knicker-nicker? Are you interrupted? If so, how do the owners respond? Do you run or offer an explanation?

2. The following outdoor sex scene comes from Iris Murdoch's *The Nice and the Good* (1970).[13]

> There was silence. The insects buzzed and whispered and behind their small patient frenzy the hot stifling air sighed with its own stillness.

Peter and Morgan were staring at each other.

'Yes,' said Peter very softly. 'Yes. That is – perfect. And – oh, Morgan –'

Morgan took off her glasses. The next moment she and Peter were locked in each other's arms.

Morgan shifted her knees, drawing the boy's body close up against her own. She could feel the firm sweaty flesh through the flimsy shirt. Her arms were locked behind his shoulders and her lips quested over his hot cheek. His hands moved upon her back, gentle at first, now suddenly violent. Their heads, pressed bone to bone, struggled for space and their lips met and remained joined. (189)

Write an outdoor sex scene, bringing in aspects of the environment to interrupt or excite. Be explicit.

3. Describe a teenager's bedroom in a way that suggests the teenager's race and gender, their decade, their personality, what sort of household or institution they live in, their socioeconomic bracket, their country or part of the country. Try not to do this solely through their posters and CDs.

## Dining rooms

A dining room scene is usually an ensemble piece, and its dialogue and description can be a challenge to orchestrate. Placements around a table are often hierarchical, with guests made keenly aware of the pecking order. In restaurants, institutions or rich homes, meals often depend on the work of invisible hands. You may, as a modern writer, feel more interested in the present and absent servants: a source of inspiration for many contemporary novelists.[14] Or you may prefer to let your characters 'graze', or enjoy a picnic, a TV dinner, a takeaway, a snack at a breakfast bar or at their desk as they work.

Formal meal times, however, can be a rich source of cultural commentary and a staple of the comedy of embarrassment (see the extract from Colm Tóibín's *The Master* [2004], in Exercises, below). If you like writing dialogue, describing food or observing social customs, you may want to include scenes from corporate entertainment, or in cafés, school dining rooms, restaurants, refectories, or above and below stairs. Those which involve an argument or clash – of classes, personalities or family values – are probably the most entertaining in fiction if not in life. Note that all three authors whose work is sampled below choose to describe their gatherings from a detached, embarrassed or dissident perspective. An interesting crowd scene is harder to describe when your point of view character is in the thick of it.

Nancy Mitford structures a chapter of *Love in a Cold Climate* (1945) round a meal in a country house.[15] Chapter 5 begins as The Honourable Frances Logan, known as Fanny, dresses for dinner, and ends with her in the Long Gallery learning to play backgammon. This extract comes from the middle:

> In the dining-room, between the man called Rory and the man called Roly, I found things even worse than I had expected. The protective colouring, which had worked so well in the drawing-room, was now going on and off like a deficient electric light. I was visible. One of my neighbours would begin a conversation with me, and seem quite interested in what I was telling him when, without any warning at all, I would become invisible and Rory and Roly were both shouting across the table at the lady called Veronica, while I was left in mid-air with some sad little remark. It then became too obvious that they had not heard a single word I had been saying but had all along been entranced by the infinitely more fascinating conversation of this Veronica lady. All right then, invisible, which really I much preferred, able to eat happily away in silence. But no, not at all, unaccountably visible again.
>
> 'Is Lord Alconleigh your uncle then? Isn't he quite barmy? Doesn't he hunt people with bloodhounds at full moon?'
>
> I was still enough of a child to accept the grown-ups of my own family without a question, and to suppose that each in their own way was more or less perfect, and it gave me a shock to hear this stranger refer to my uncle as quite barmy.
>
> 'Oh, but we love it,' I began, 'you can't imagine what fun – ' No good. Even as I spoke I became invisible'. (173–74)

Our first-person narrator has recently 'come out' and is therefore officially adult. Such dinner parties, however, contribute to an extended and sometimes painful rite of passage. Though Fanny takes her privilege for granted, Mitford maintains reader sympathy for her heroine by keeping her naivety to the fore, and by her modest description of herself as a 'deficient electric light' (173). Later in the dinner, when guests are vying for power, Mitford will give us tracts of witty direct speech. Note that here, however, she contrives to communicate babble with few verbatim examples, sustaining pace by her deft use of summary and adding humour through Fanny's divergent viewpoint.

Note also how Mitford introduces and builds an important character not through speech and gesture but through other people's responses. The 'Veronica lady' says almost nothing yet Mitford convinces us of her wit and appeal – in upper-class circles, at least – by the reactions of 'Rory and Roly' and other equally interchangeable guests. Direct speech, as when Fanny is asked if her uncle is 'quite barmy', seems all the more intrusive. Though we never doubt Fanny's – or Mitford's – involvement in this society, Mitford makes the young Fanny naïvely defensive, thus giving us a clear-cut take on its crassness and vanity.

The characters in Helen Simpson's short story 'Café Society' (2000) are not upper but middle class: two women and an unruly child.[16] Note how Simpson uses a public space to convey a society as well as an epoch in her characters' lives:

> [Sally and Frances] might have gone to McDonald's, so cheap and tolerant, packed with flat light and fat smells and unofficial crèche clamour. There they could have slumped like the old punchbags they are while Ben screeched and flew around with the other children. McDonald's is essentially a wordless experience, though, and they both want to see if they can for a wonder exchange some words. Then there is Pete's café on the main road, a lovely steamy unbuttoned room where men sit in their work clothes in a friendly fug of bonhomie and banter, smoking, stirring silver streams of sugar into mugs of bright brown tea. But it would not be fair to take this child in there and spoil that Edenic all-day-breakfast fun. It would take the insensitivity of an ox. Unthinkable. [ . . . ]
>
> Ben takes the buttery knife from the side of his plate and waves it in the air, then drops it onto his mother's coat sleeve. From there it falls to her lap and then, noisily, to the floor. She dabs at the butter stains with a tissue and bangs her forehead as she reaches beneath the table for the knife. Ben laughs and sandpapers his chin with a square of toast. (11–12)

As travesties of an ideal repast, fictional meals are often used to lay desire bare. Mitford's heroine Fanny was dreading 'this grown-up dinner' and wished at the start of the chapter that she could have her supper on a tray in the schoolroom with her friend (173). Sally and Frances 'hope to talk, for their minds to meet', though they know 'the odds against this happening are about fifty to one' (10). The café where they drink their 'powerless cappuccinos' and which displays 'metal trays of damp cheese, dead ham and tired old tuna mixed with sweetcorn kernels' is as much a gendered space as the kitchen at the Heights or in *Love* (16). Its opposite is another, imagined scene: the cosily sensuous room where working men sit and where women with noisy children dare not intrude.

Mitford's central character is her first-person narrator, whereas Simpson chooses an omniscient ('all-knowing') viewpoint. You may associate this with Victorian complacency or some sort of 'God-like' stance. If so, study this story and analyse the flexibility of Simpson's technique. It enables her, for example, to state objectively what is happening, as when she describes the fate of the buttery knife. It also allows her to tell us what each character looks like; and sometimes what they both look like at once, as when they sit, 'po-faced, glum, gazing at zany Ben as he stabs holes into the police rabbit with a sharp red pen' (17). Simpson can also dive into the mind of either woman to reveal her past and sometimes even her future, mainly through long, italicized passages limning in private thoughts.

Yet far from feeling chilly or detached, Simpson's authorial voice is one of sympathy for the women. This is partly because her observations are detailed and acute: 'This woman Sally has a drinker's face, but her lustreless grey skin and saurian eye come not from alcohol but from prolonged lack of sleep'; and partly because she – unlike some eighteenth- and nineteenth-century authors – seldom utters general 'truths' or pronounces on her characters' deserts (12).

## Dining room exercises

1. The following dinner scene comes from Colm Tóibín's novel, *The Master* (2004), about the novelist, Henry James, and is written from Henry's third person limited viewpoint.[17] It is set in his home in Rye. Lily Norton is his guest, Smith his butler and Burgess Noakes a servant.

> Smith opened the door with Burgess Noakes in view behind him. Burgess was wearing a jacket which was much too large for him. He had the look of a tramp. Smith carried a plate of meat with the movements of someone who was about to expire. Burgess followed behind with other plates. Lily Norton turned and studied them, and in one second Henry watched her grasp what was happening at Lamb House. All her subtlety and self-control failed her. She seemed most sharply alarmed, and her smile when she turned away from the two servants was forced. Smith at that moment began to pour more wine into her glass but could not keep his hand steady. The other three watched him helplessly as he allowed some of the wine to spill and then, as he tried to correct himself, poured a quantity of wine directly onto the table-cloth. When he turned from the table, his movements became a set of doddering, staggery steps as he left the room, abandoning the serving of the meal to Burgess Noakes. (218)

Describe an embarrassing meal when events spiral out of the host's or hostess's control. What hinges on the occasion? How do the guests respond? Who is (are) your point of view character(s)?

2. Describe a meal in detail from the viewpoint of a cook or chef who has gone to considerable trouble. Is she at home or in a restaurant? What is on the menu? Do her recipes work? What do they say about her personality or economic status? What happens when one of the guests claims they have a dangerous allergy to a major ingredient?

## Notes

1. W. Shakespeare, *A Midsummer Night's Dream*, Act V, i, 17.
2. V. Nabokov, *Lectures on Literature*, ed. F. Bowers (New York and London: Harcourt Brace Jovanovich, 1980), p. 185.
3. B. E. Ellis, *American Psycho* (London: Picador, 1991).
4. D. Means, *The Secret Goldfish* (London: Fourth Estate, 2004).
5. E. Brontë, *Wuthering Heights* (New York: Norton Critical edn, 1972).
6. T. Morrison, *Love* (London: Chatto & Windus, 2003).
7. T. Morrison, *Beloved* (London: Chatto & Windus, 1987).
8. M. Roberts, *During Mother's Absence* (London: Virago, 1993).
9. E. M. Forster, *Maurice* (London: Penguin, 1975).
10. D. B. C. Pierre, *Vernon God Little* (London: Faber and Faber, 2003).
11. C. Brontë, *Jane Eyre* (New York: Norton Critical edn, 1987).
12. F. Scott Fitzgerald, *The Great Gatsby* (London: Penguin, 1995).
13. I. Murdoch, *The Nice and the Good* (London: Penguin, 1972).
14. See, for example, J. Rhys's *Wide Sargasso Sea* (1966) which describes, among other characters, the Caribbean domestic staff of the first Mrs Rochester; V. Martin's *Mary Reilly* (1990) which retells the story of R. L. Stevenson's *Dr Jekyll and Mr Hyde* (1886) from the point of view of a servant, anonymous and only once mentioned in the original; and M. Forster's *Lady's Maid* (1990) which narrates the love story of Robert Browning and Elizabeth Barrett from the perspective of the latter's maid.
15. N. Mitford, *Love in a Cold Climate* (London: Penguin, 2000).
16. H. Simpson, *Hey Yeah Right Get a Life* (London: Jonathan Cape, 2000).
17. C. Tóibín, *The Master* (London: Picador, 2004).

# 12

# Bodily States

## Linda Anderson

Have you ever wept over the fate of a fictional character or cheered at their triumphs? Have you become so involved with their predicaments that you have sat on the edge of your seat while they were in trouble? Maybe you have even wished you could go on a date with one of them? These are such common reading pleasures that we forget how astonishing it is that writers can conjure up characters who seem like living, breathing people, real enough to make us care about them.

How is it done? One answer lies in the ability to imagine and convey characters' bodily lives. For example, look at the following novel extract which describes a young teacher's first experience of her job. As you read, notice the number of allusions to actual bodily states.

> By the afternoon the combination of her intermittent sweat and the air-conditioning had taken its toll: she stank slightly, and wished she'd worn a cardigan over her T-shirt to hide the patches under her arms. The problem she thought would be to keep the children quiet. In fact, she couldn't get them to talk: row upon row of fourteen-year-olds, asleep or terrified or sullenly resentful, appeared before her; and she guessed in retrospect that she should have waited them out. But at the time – how could it be otherwise, given the restless, eager, dissatisfied current to her nature – she buzzed and flitted around them, playing the fool or the prim miss as the occasion demanded, confusing them and herself, desiring alternately and with an instant passion that surprised her to be each of their best friends or never to see them again. By eleven thirty

she was utterly beat. She sat in the stall in the teachers' WC and cried. Then composed her face, and walked out across the baseball field on a bright clear September day whose sunshine it seemed couldn't touch her as she shivered in it regardless, heading for the cafeteria. The sight of all those children talking at once and eating appalled her. Already she suffered from a kind of persistent stage fright, convinced she would be called upon to remember a name or chastise a delinquent. So she held her head up in a blind way, certain that everyone could see what a miserable fraud she was.[1]

The first piece of physical information is forthright and jolting: 'she stank' immediately gives us the sense of her mortified self-consciousness. Her vision of the pupils is almost hallucinatory: 'row upon row of fourteen-year-olds [ . . . ] appeared before her'. She sweats visibly indoors but later shivers outside despite the sunlight. She 'buzzes' and 'flits' around her pupils, full of nervous energy. She is suddenly 'beat', which seems to mean both exhausted and defeated. She cries in the toilet. She sees the pupils dining together and is again overcome with fright at their sheer numbers. Her body is a battleground as she tries to put on an act, sometimes playing the 'fool or the prim miss', or trying to regain her composure by controlling her face and holding her head high.

It would be possible to write this piece in a more 'interior' way, focusing on the workings of her mind rather than this constant interplay of mind and body, but it would be a lot less powerful. We would lose the tension of the conflict between how she wants to appear and the helpless 'leakage' of her true feelings as revealed by her body. We would also find it harder to 'see' her. Whether you have ever been in a similar predicament to this character or not, you will readily recognize her feelings because everyone knows what it is like to sweat and shiver, to feel strung out and exhausted, or to try to overcome an attack of 'nerves'.

The aim of this chapter is to encourage you to develop convincing characters by creating a strong sense of their physical beings and surroundings as well as their inner lives. Everything that you understand or imagine about other people begins with your own experience. We'll look first at how you can draw on your own bodily experiences and memories and ascribe them to fictional characters. This is not to suggest that you can only write what you know or must be restricted to creating characters similar to yourself. Far from it. We'll look later in the chapter at how to imagine characters who are different from you physically (perhaps in age, size or sex) or who have done things that you may have never experienced, anything from giving birth to bungee-jumping.

## Exercise

Using yourself.
Make a list of 10 intense physical experiences you have had. For example, here are the kinds of things you might include,

- Repetitive work on a factory line.
- Travel sickness.
- Giving birth.
- Falling in love with someone's voice.
- Being part of a festive crowd.
- A dramatic haircut or restyle.
- Learning the tango.
- Climbing winding stairs in a tower.
- Being a pallbearer at a funeral.
- Singing in a choir.

When you have made your own list, select the experience that interests you most at the moment. Write an account of it including as much sensory detail as you can about the sights, sounds or smells you remember as well as what you thought and felt, so that you show the impact of the experience on your body and mind. Use up to 200 words.

Read over what you have written and think about whether you could ascribe that experience or some part of it to any fictional character you are currently developing. If not, save it and add others to it so that you have a fund of descriptions that you might make use of in stories at some point.

These descriptions do not always need to be of special or momentous events. Details of small, ordinary observations will also be useful: the exact colour of a sky at twilight; the scent of your child's hair; the scratchiness of a rough scarf round your neck; the dizzying onset of flu; the rasping feel of a cat's tongue; the taste of day-old beer; the discreet morning sound of a milk-float. Get into the habit of recording what you observe around you and raiding your notebook for authentic details that will help make your characters 'real'.

## Translating your experiences

Your use of your own experience does not always have to be straight-forward. If you need to describe something unfamiliar, you can search your experience for a plausible equivalent and draw on that. For example, I recently interviewed the novelist Andrew Greig for an Open University course CD about techniques for writing fiction. We discussed his bestselling novel, *That Summer*, which is set at the time of the Battle of Britain and deals mainly with the impact of the war upon a young couple, Stella, who works as a radar operator, and Len, who is a fighter pilot.[2] One of the achievements of this novel is to capture the mood of the times, the heightened sense of being alive experienced by people surrounded by carnage and the threat of extinction. This is what Andrew Greig said about how he managed to write the flying combat scenes:

> I've never flown a plane in my life and I've certainly not flown in combat! But what you do is you find something of yours that's equivalent and I used to do this rather frightening rock and ice climbing and I remembered that extraordinary sense of immediacy of being alive, of alternating terror, relief and exhilaration that came from climbing; the way that time slows and then goes very fast. I just translated that emotional psychological thing that I did know about into that situation. So I think there are many professions or situations that you cannot have experienced yourself but you find an equivalent that you feel translates.[3]

Many writers have used their knowledge of the disciplines and processes of the writing life itself to invent characters involved in other arts: for example, Siri Hustvedt has written about a male artist in *What I Loved*[4] and Bernard MacLaverty has portrayed a female musical composer in *Grace Notes*.[5] In my own case, I've drawn on my childhood memory of being confined to bed for weeks with an illness to write a woman prisoner in one of my novels, transposing the boredom and sense of entrapment to a different character and situation.

Think about your job or profession, your sports, hobbies and other experiences and see whether you could use any of them as a way into imagining unfamiliar activities that your characters might undertake. Note down anything that occurs to you.

## Body–mind conflicts

We have already seen in the extract about the young teacher that a conflict between body and mind can generate dramatic tension. It can even fuel a whole story.

Here is another example of a work dilemma, a factual first-person account of a harsh job in a plastics factory written by Luc Sante. The job entailed 'repeating a chain of actions four times a minute over seven and a half hours − 1,800 times a day' in conditions of 'broiling heat', 'poisonous and unmoving air', 'bad light' and 'punishing din'.[6] The writer describes the effect of the mechanical work on his body:

> After a day or two I had absorbed the machine's rhythm. As I fell asleep every night in my bed I could feel each muscle group involved in the cycle going through its paces in sequence, again and again. (119)

He fought back against the excruciating boredom by singing and by reciting poetry, but soon exhausted his repertoire. He decided to try and read:

> I arranged my space for maximum efficiency, moving the boxes to the other side of the grinder so that I could pack product with one hand while discarding excess with the other. Having pared my movements down to the strict minimum I had enough time between one cycle and the next to read about half a sentence. I tried crime novels but kept losing my place. Finally I had a stroke of inspiration. Only one author would do: Céline. His works [ . . . ] were all spat out in brief angry bursts separated by ellipses. The solution was perfect. Not only did I have exactly the time required to read one such particule between every two cycles of the machine, but their emotional content might have been designed for the circumstances. (119)

In the original example, the teacher's body resists her attempts to perform poise and authority. In Sante's account of his job, it is his mind that revolts against the way his body is being reduced to a slaving replica of the machine. Either way, pitting mind and body against each other is an excellent way to produce drama and suspense.

## Exercise

Write about an intense physical experience you have had which has created a strong conflict between your mind and body. Check your earlier list to see if there is a suitable one there; otherwise find something new. It might be a time when you forced yourself to do a job you hated or followed orders reluctantly. It might be a time when you had to complete a task despite being ill or had to be charming to someone you disliked. Show the struggle between mind and body without explaining it.

For example, instead of 'I hated my boss because he treated me with suspicion', say something like, 'Every time I looked up, my boss's eyes were on me and the look in those eyes was never benign'. Use up to 200 words.

## Walking in other people's shoes

One of the joys of writing fiction is the scope it gives us to invent characters who may be very different from ourselves, to live multiple lives in our imaginations. In her essay 'On Being Ill', Virginia Woolf has written about this imaginative capacity, which is common in children but often lost later.

> There is no harm in choosing to live over and over, now as a man, now as a woman, as sea-captain, or court lady, as Emperor or farmer's wife, in splendid cities and on remote moors, at the time of Pericles or Arthur, Charlemagne, or George the Fourth – to live and live till we have lived out those embryo lives which attend about us in early youth until I 'suppressed them'.[7]

How do you go about creating someone unlike yourself, perhaps radically so? It's important to be bold about this matter of impersonation, not to put yourself off by thinking that you couldn't possibly write someone of the opposite sex, for example, or someone a lot younger or older than yourself. That kind of belief is self-fulfilling and so is the opposite one. You can empower yourself by having faith in your ability to invent a wide range of characters.

In practical terms, you need to approach each new character with a combination of empathy, imagination and sometimes research, say, in the case of an historical figure or someone in a profession you know little about. It will pay to spend time building up a full picture of your character – they will rarely burst into your mind full-fledged.

Starting with the body is one of the most powerful ways to identify strongly with a character. Are your characters comfortable or unhappy in their own skins? Are they proud of one of their physical attributes? Do they draw attention to it in some way? Or do they try to conceal some aspect of their body? Think about how a person's history is inscribed on his or her body – signs of ageing, scars, stretch marks, loss of teeth. The body itself can be a storehouse of memory or a marker of identity.

Do your characters have any physical difficulties or disabilities? Eczema, short-sightedness, back pain, impaired hearing? Think about the effect of any physical vulnerability on their self-image and behaviour.

Do your characters have any physical distinctions or gifts? For example, as mentioned earlier, Bernard MacLaverty's *Grace Notes* is about a woman composer, Catherine McKenna, who was raised as a Northern Irish Catholic. The author has made her someone in whom the auditory sense is predominant. She translates experience into musical terms to create a 'world in sound – a kind of aural atlas' (36). This includes her own body when she describes her pulse as 'the body's metronome' or her pregnant belly as a Lambeg drum (41). At the start of the novel, as she returns home for her father's funeral, she remembers an early act of resistance against the standard tribal responses which he tried to transmit to her. Her father would rail against local Orangemen whose drumming matches on huge Lambeg drums would create a thunderous menacing rumble as if the whole town were 'under a canopy of dark noise' (7). He condemned the drummers as 'bowler-hatted dunderheads' driven by 'sheer bloody bigotry' (8, 9). But Catherine thrilled to the sound and tried to analyse it dispassionately:

> She tried to keep time with her toes inside her shoes. There were slaps and dunts on the off-beats, complex rhythms she couldn't begin to write down – even now, never mind then. The two sticks working independently. The hands tripping each other up. A ripple bouncing back and interfering with the other ripples which had first started it. The drums were battered so loud she felt the vibrations in her body, was sure the sky and the air about her were pounding to the beat. It didn't exactly make her want to dance, more to sway. (8, 9)

Her physical gift also reveals and reinforces her independent spirit which spurred her in adulthood to subvert a male-dominated musical order. The physical is not merely physical – it suggests the person's emotional and mental life.

Visualize your characters strongly – see how they stand, move, shake hands or eat. Overhear their speech and how this may change in different contexts or moods. Try writing your characters' diary entries or letters to capture their way of thinking and writing.

When you have established a strong sense of your character's body and bodily life, you can deepen your identification by using some of the methods actors use. For example, 'the hot seat' game, which is sometimes used in rehearsals. Actors take turns at being interviewed in character. They must answer probing questions like 'Are you satisfied with your marriage?', 'What made you choose your job?', 'What are your hopes for your daughter?'. If they do not already know an answer, they have to reach for it then and there and this can deepen their discoveries about the character. If you have the opportunity to work with other writers, try playing the hot seat game. Alternatively, you might try writing a full history of your character as actors do in the Stanislavski Method as a way of identifying closely with them in order to produce a compelling performance. You can try out experiences you have not had and empathize with characters you don't know. With practice, you will be able to enter with conviction into the mind and voice even of characters you dislike or condemn.

## Exercise

Over the next week, start creating two or three characters you might use in stories later. Use the questionnaire and either of the methods outlined above to flesh out your characters with as much detail as possible. Work in short bursts of 10–15 minutes.

### Bodily transformations

People's bodies mediate and control their life stories and their bodies are subject to constant change. Just think of the many possible categories of change:

- Birth, puberty, maturation, ageing, death.
- Pregnancy, menopause.
- Illness, medical interventions, processes of recovery.
- Intoxication.
- Self-decoration: cosmetics, tattoos.
- Cosmetic surgery.
- Disfigurements caused by accident or illness.
- Disabilities or lessening powers, for example failing eyesight.
- Theatrical changes and disguises, for example celebrity look-alikes.
- Gaining and losing weight.
- Impacts upon the body of work, love, class, religion, gender 'rules'.

These processes of transformation, whether joyous or fearful, can form the theme or 'plot' of whole stories or novels. Take the scenario of a sudden announcement of serious illness. This is the powerful 'engine' of a lot of fiction. For example, in John Updike's story

'Poker Night', a man is told by his doctor that he has cancer.[8] He decides to keep his regular appointment with some friends who play poker together. He doesn't tell them his news but, of course, it affects him throughout the evening: he notices the poignant signs of ageing in the other men, their 'old guys' hands, withered long wrinkled white claws with spots and grey hair and stand-up veins' (154). His love for his friends wells up: '[ . . . ] my throat began to go rough, they were all so damn sweet, and I'd known them so damn long, without ever saying much of anything except this clowning around and whose deal was it; maybe that was the sweetness' (154). It is only when he gets home that he divulges the news – to his wife Alma, and even though she says and does all the right things, the man feels cut off and comfortless: 'But she wasn't me. I was me' (155).

## Exercise

Take the line quoted above ('But she wasn't me. I was me') and use it in a story centred on a different bodily predicament. For example, you might invent a character who is reluctantly pregnant or someone who emerges from an illness with a new set of values. Or invent your own scenario.

### Miraculous transformations

Magical realist fiction often contains fabulous alterations to characters' bodies. Isabel Allende's *The House of the Spirits* combines the everyday and the marvellous so matter-of-factly that we glide easily into acceptance of characters with green hair, the gift of prophecy or the ability to fly.[9] In Angela Carter's penultimate novel, *Nights at the Circus*, the central character is a world-famous winged woman Fevvers, a trapeze artist who tells her life story to a journalist.[10] He initially wants to expose her as a fraud but becomes enchanted with her and joins the circus as a clown. Although the story is a comic fable, Fevvers's wings have an important symbolic dimension. The novel is set in 1899, a period when agitation for women's rights began to emerge. When Fevvers first spreads her wings, Ma Nelson, the mistress of the brothel where Fevvers spent her childhood, declares that she is 'the pure child of the century that just now is waiting in the wings, the New Age in which no women will be bound down to the ground' (25). Ma Nelson stops Fevvers from playing Cupid in the brothel and gets her to pose as Winged Victory. But the symbolism is not allowed to reduce Fevvers to an icon. She is also a real, individual woman with faults and appetites, someone who gorges and stuffs herself with food and dreams of bank accounts.

## Exercise

Imagine an 'ordinary' character, male or female, who begins to grow wings. It starts with an itch in the shoulder blades, and then something sinewy and feathery begins to sprout. How does your character respond and how does s/he cope? How do others react? What does the transformation mean, if anything?

### Writing sex

Czech novelist Milan Kundera said once in a television interview that writing sex scenes was one of the greatest artistic and moral challenges for a writer. If that's not daunting enough, every year in Britain *The Literary Review* hands out its Bad Sex Award, which has been won by some illustrious writers. The award was established to try and stamp out 'unnecessary, inept and embarrassing' sex scenes in literature. Leaving aside the fact that in real life sex itself may sometimes be unnecessary, inept and embarrassing, how can we avoid writing cringe-making sex scenes?

First, if there is no good reason to include a description of love-making, don't. But if your story requires one, then it's best to write it without imagining your parents reading it. And then avoid the main pitfalls:

- Mechanical descriptions and overused words like 'thrust', 'moist', 'groaned' and so on.
- Florid and reverential language ('She saw all the colours of the rainbow', 'She had never known such perfect bliss').
- Euphemism ('He relieved the tautness in himself').

Desire rarely makes people sensible and a lot of good comic writing is based on the self-deception of amorous characters. For example, in Frank Ronan's *A Picnic in Eden*, vain, handsome Iain MacLeod goes home with plain, forceful Annie Millar. She is completely repulsed by him:

> She kept her eyes shut and regretted having brought him back. She had thought that good looks would be a guarantee of something, and she thought that he would be cool and hard and alien. Instead she found herself being slobbered and sweated on.[11]

Meanwhile, Iain has fallen in love and believes that she must have too.

> When he flung off his clothes and stood before her like one of those idiots painted by William Blake, he thought that she averted her eyes because of the blinding light that emanated from his flesh. When she pushed him away with a shudder he thought that he had worn her out with his passion and she could take no more. When he wiped himself on the sheet he thought that he was leaving her a gift to remember him by. He thought that while he slept she would be watching his face through the night, longing to touch it, but afraid of waking him. (7)

The originality of this piece is to do with the choice of an omniscient narrator telling us with great asperity about the mismatched feelings of the man and the woman. There is also the surprise of a handsome man falling for a plain and charmless woman. The story becomes more sombre subsequently. He stays in thrall to her and is destroyed by her indifference.

Another surprising depiction of sex is in Toni Morrison's *Sula*.[12] Childless and unmarried, Sula is viewed in her community as a pariah because of her promiscuity.

> She went to bed with men as frequently as she could. It was the only place where she could find what she was looking for: misery and the ability to feel deep sorrow. She had not always been aware that it was sadness that she yearned for. Lovemaking seemed to her, at first, the creation of a special kind of joy. She thought she liked the sootiness of sex and its comedy; she laughed a great deal during the raucous beginnings, and rejected those lovers who regarded sex as healthy or beautiful. Sexual aesthetics bored her. Although she did not regard sex as ugly (ugliness was boring also), she liked to think of it as wicked. But as her experiences multiplied she realized that not only was it not wicked, it was not necessary for her to conjure up the idea of wickedness in order to participate fully. During the lovemaking she found and needed to find the cutting edge. When she left off co-operating with her body and began to assert herself in the act, particles of strength gathered in her like steel shavings drawn to a spacious magnetic centre, forming a tight cluster that nothing, it seemed, could break. And there was utmost irony and outrage in lying under someone, in a position of surrender, feeling her own abiding strength and limitless power. But the cluster did break, fall apart and in her panic to hold it together she leaped from the edge into soundlessness and went down howling, howling in a stinging awareness of the endings of things: an eye of sorrow in the midst of all the hurricane of joy. (122–23)

'Casual' sex turns out here not to be shallow at all. It is Sula's way of connecting to a desolating awareness of mortality and a compassion for the fragility of all existence. It is her particular way of having sex. What Morrison and Ronan have both done is to link sex deeply with character and, in that way, achieve a sense of sexual response unique to their characters. It seems that the way to write something surprising might be not to chase after surprise for its own sake, but to be true to your characters.

## Conclusion

Being true to your characters is, in fact, the single most important strategy in creating believable characters that readers will care about. This means that you will need to take your time to get to know your characters. Put in the groundwork. Make daring experiments in using characters different from yourself and your immediate circle. As American author Joyce Carol Oates said,

> For is biology destiny? Not for the writer or artist, it isn't.[13]

## Notes

1. B. Markovits, *Either Side of Winter* (London: Faber and Faber, 2005), p. 16.
2. A. Greig, *That Summer* (London: Faber and Faber, 2000).
3. A. Greig in conversation with the Open University. Unpublished transcript of interview (2006).
4. S. Hustvedt, *What I Loved* (London: Sceptre, 2003).
5. B. MacLaverty, *Grace Notes* (London: Jonathan Cape, 1997).
6. L. Sante, 'Plastics', *Granta: The Factory*, 89 (2005), pp. 113–24.
7. V. Woolf, 'On Being Ill', quoted by H. Lee, 'Prone to fancy', *Guardian*, 18th December 2004, p. 11.
8. J. Updike, 'Poker Night', *Trust Me: Stories* (London: Penguin Books, 1988 [1987]).
9. I. Allende, *The House of the Spirits* (London: Everyman's Library, 2005 [1985]).
10. A. Carter, *Nights at the Circus* (London: Picador, 1985).
11. F. Ronan, *A Picnic in Eden* (London: Bloomsbury, 1991).
12. T. Morrison, *Sula* (London: Chatto & Windus, 1988 [1974]).
13. J. C. Oates, 'The Importance of Childhood', *The Writing Life*, ed. M. Arana (New York: Public Affairs, 2003), p. 18.

# 13

# Writing the Landscape

## Lee Martin

American rocker, John Mellencamp, calls Bloomington, Indiana, home. For those of you unfamiliar with the geography of the United States, Bloomington is what we'd call 'a hop, skip, and a jump' from where I grew up just over the state line in the agricultural land of southern Illinois.

'No, I cannot forget from where it is I come from,' Mellencamp sings in his 1985 song, 'Small Town,' and because we're practically neighbors – because we share the landscape of the rural Midwest – I forgive him the clunky repetition of the preposition in that line.[1] I understand the sentiment; we are tied to places. Sometimes they're the places of our births, as is the case for John and me, and sometimes they're adopted landscapes, found later in life, as happened for another John, my friend, novelist and short-story writer, John Dufresne, who grew up in Worcester, Massachusetts, but who has lived for over 20 years now in the southern states of Louisiana and Florida which often provide the setting for his fiction. Whether by birthright or adoption, fiction writers cozy up to particular landscapes and use them to give their writing authority, contribute to characterization, suggest plots, and influence tone and atmosphere.

### The lifeline between fiction and place

When we write about the places we know intimately, our fiction is fuller on every level. We see our characters more completely, we let them and their richly rendered details suggest plots, and we work at a level of language that organically grows from the place and its connection to our minds and hearts. 'The truth is,' Eudora Welty wrote in her essay, 'Place in Fiction,' 'fiction depends for its life on place.'[2]

Often, you'll hear writers say – all right, I'll admit it; I've said it myself more than once – that they begin with character. Something about a particular character catches their fancy; perhaps it's an interesting contradiction within that character or a surprising action that requires a story or maybe a novel to figure out the why of that action. Why, for example, would a boy climb onto the roof of a synagogue and refuse to come down, as happens in Philip Roth's story, 'The Conversion of the Jews.'[3] It takes Roth's story, with its dramatization of the tensions between religious faith and personal identity to attempt an answer. It's absolutely true that writers are interested in the mysteries of people, what William Faulkner called 'the old verities and truths of the heart.'[4] If we look more closely, though, at where characters begin to form, we find that, as in real life, people take shape the way they do in part because of the place they occupy. Landscape is any fiction writer's starting point. Stories and novels unfold, or should, from particular geographical locations and the precise, vivid presentation of those landscapes gives the writing an undeniable authority.

Take, for example, the opening paragraph of Sarah Orne Jewett's story, 'A White Heron':

> The woods were already filled with shadows one June evening, just before eight o'clock, though a bright sunset still glimmered faintly among the trunks of the trees. A little girl was driving home her cow, a plodding, dilatory, provoking creature in her behavior, but a valued companion for all that. They were going away from the western light, and striking deep into the dark woods, but their feet were familiar with the path, and it was no matter whether their eyes could see it or not.[5]

The first line announces immediately that here is a writer completely familiar with her landscape; here is a trusted guide. Though it may seem a small thing, hardly noticed on first reading, the precise description of the setting sun casting a glimmer of light on the tree trunks establishes the writer's authority. That detail convinces us that the place – those woods into which the little girl drives her cow – is real, and if the place is real, the people are real and everything that happens in the story is authentic. If asked to write a description of a New England woods just before eight o'clock on a June evening, how many of us would use that detail of the faint light on the tree trunks? Not many, I'd wager, unless at some point we'd spent time in such a place and if our powers of observation were so sharp that we could recall that unique detail. Joseph Conrad once said of his work, 'My task which I am trying to achieve is, by the power of the written word, to make you hear, to make you feel, it is, above all, to make you see. That – and no more, and it is everything.'[6] A writer's vision of a place often comes through the use of a well-placed and precise detail. Writer and reader alike dream what John Gardner, in *The Art of Fiction*, calls 'the fictional dream,'[7] and, as we're immersed in the setting of a story or novel, we become like the little girl 'striking deep into the dark woods,' well-acquainted with the path.

Much like filmmakers, fiction writers have at their disposal a variety of 'shots' when they describe landscape. All of them contribute not only to the fictional dream in the reader's mind but also to the writer's authority as well as to the story that will emerge from the world portrayed. The single important detail such as the light on the tree trunks that carries such weight in the opening line from the Jewett story is a slightly different visual technique than the one John Steinbeck uses in the opening paragraph of his story, 'The Chrysanthemums':

> The high grey-flannel fog of winter closed off the Salinas Valley from the sky and from all the rest of the world. On every side it sat like a lid on the mountains and made of the great valley a closed pot. On the broad, level land floor the gang plows bit deep and left the black earth shining like metal where the shares had cut. On the foothill ranches across the Salinas River, the yellow stubble fields seemed to be bathed in pale cold sunshine, but there was no sunshine in the valley now in December. The thick willow scrub along the river flamed with sharp and positive yellow leaves.[8]

Steinbeck uses a lens with a wider angle than Jewett does in the opening of 'The White Heron.' 'The Chrysanthemums' begins with a description of California's Salinas Valley from a distant vantage point. We're able to see the fog that settles 'like a lid on the mountains,' the land floors scarred by plows, the foothill ranches with their 'yellow stubble fields,' and 'the thick willow scrub along the river.' We see sky, mountain, valley, field, and river. A wide shot indeed, but notice how within that shot Steinbeck finds, much the way Jewett does, a single, sharp detail that – because we could not have predicted it, and certainly wouldn't have been able to conjure it up ourselves – has the ring of authenticity that tells us how well this writer knows the landscape he describes. I'm talking about the description of 'the black earth shining like metal where the shares had cut.' Only someone familiar with such a place would know that the earth, turned up in a furrow, has that metallic sheen to it. Remember what Conrad said about how making a reader see is everything. Here Steinbeck lets us see a more panoramic view of the landscape before narrowing his lens to show us the characters who will emerge from that setting and how their actions and consequences will be inextricable from the place in which they occur.

A writer also establishes authority by remembering the importance of using a variety of sensory details in the evocation of landscape. We tend to think most often of description in terms of the visual, but we mustn't forget that setting can take on even more dimension and significance when other senses enter into the portrait. Often, we see more fully and powerfully if we 'see' through what we hear, smell, taste, and touch. For example, Stephen Dobyns opens his story, 'Kansas,' with a boy hitchhiking on a back-country dirt road on a cloudless day in July. A farmer in a pickup truck finally gives him a ride. Notice how Dobyns uses more than the visual details to give this moment authenticity:

> The farmer had light blue eyes and there was stubble on his chin. Perhaps he was forty, but to the boy he looked old. His skin was leather-colored from the sun. The farmer pressed his foot to the floor and the pickup roared. It was a dirt road and the boy had to hold his hands against the dashboard to keep from being bounced around. It was hot and both windows were open. There was grit in the boy's eyes and on his tongue.[9]

After a clear visual image of the farmer (blue eyes, beard stubble, leathery skin), Dobyns gives the moment sound (the roar of the truck), motion (the boy has to brace himself to keep from being jostled as the truck bounces over the dirt road), tactility (hot air rushing in through the open truck windows, the grit from dust in the boy's eyes), and taste (that same grit on the boy's tongue). The combination of the sensory details fully immerses us in the scene, and we're quite willing to follow Dobyns wherever he chooses to take us.

Some landscapes, of course, are more dramatic with natural beauty than others – mountains, oceans, the Amazon rainforest – but the fact remains that no matter how urban, homogenous, or mundane a setting may appear at first glance, it always contains details that not only provide vivid description but also establish the writer as an authority, someone with the intimate knowledge necessary to tell the story that the landscapes contain. It's our job as writers to put our observation skills to work to find the telling details, the ones that convince a reader that the narrative really comes from that place and could only come from there because the characters and the incidents are so firmly connected to the landscape.

## Nothing happens nowhere

Too often, our early attempts at fiction shortchange the importance of place by settling for the generic. A story set in a bar, for example, could be set in any bar anywhere in the world. The corner drug store could be on a street corner in Yazoo City, Mississippi, or Chicago, Illinois. Nothing distinguishes it; consequently, the place and the story happening there seem not to exist at all.

When my wife and I started looking for a house in Columbus, our real estate agent told us the most popular home was the two-story, four bedroom, two-and-a-half bath model. These homes, each done by various volume builders, indeed follow essentially the same floor plan. We saw a good number of these houses, enough to soon know what to expect: living room, dining room, kitchen opening up to the family room, four bedrooms upstairs. Still, as we made our tour, we saw enough idiosyncratic details to illustrate that, though the houses were basically the same, the lives of the current owners that went on in them were unique. The clothes hanging in the master bedroom closet in one house, for example, were all in dry cleaner's plastic. The linen closet in the hallway held stacks of towels, washcloths, sheets, blankets – all of them white.

I thought of all the people who might pass by that house on any given day – walking their dogs or driving down that street – and dismiss that house as one like all the others, never knowing about the clothes so neatly wrapped in plastic or the white linens, so sterile, sealed away in their closet. Those details, to the fiction writer, have an organic connection to the culture of the landscape, that Midwestern flatness where the land, in the 1800s, was divided into townships, each further divided into square sections. Fly over that landscape today, and from the plane you'll see the patchwork quilt effect, the land neat and orderly in its collection of squares. Roads and streets run at right angles here. We exist on a grid. I've even known towns where the original east/west streets were identified by letters, and the north/south streets by numbers. In many ways, we're a 'by the numbers' culture. What speaks more plainly about that fact than those clothes in their plastic or that linen closet full of everything white?

My point is this: people either accept the influence the landscape has on them or they resist it. Either way, stories are born. The good fiction writer knows that specific places give rise to specific characters and the plots that their actions create. Steinbeck's 'The Chrysanthemums' serves as an excellent example of this organic unity of place, character, and plot. That Salinas Valley, closed off with the low-hanging winter fog, presents a cloudy gloom and with it a particular atmosphere: 'It was a time of quiet and of waiting' (1206). Carrying that feeling of imprisonment and inertia with her is our main character, Elisa, a rancher's wife who is cutting back her chrysanthemums at the end of their season. When a tinker arrives in his wagon to ask directions, she responds to his description of his traveling from Seattle to San Diego and back every year, following nice weather. She tells him: 'That sounds like a nice way to live' (1209). Later, she adds, 'I wish women could do such things' (1211). All her loneliness and all the frustration that she feels from being locked into her role as a housewife arise naturally from the atmosphere that Steinbeck creates when he so vividly describes the landscape. The emotional landscape of her inner life then finds expression in the give and take with the tinker.

It is impossible to separate setting, character, and plot, even if a character resists the culture of a place (as is the case in a story I looked at in my chapter on 'Children in Fiction' (Chapter 11): John Updike's 'A & P').[10] Sammy, a teenager, working as a grocery clerk in a New England village defends three girls who walk into the A & P wearing bathing suits. To us today, this may seem ordinary, but at that time and in that place, the girls have definitely violated decorum. When Lengel, the store manager, makes the girls leave because they aren't decently dressed, Sammy feels so bad for them that he quits his job. He walks out into the parking lot, looking for the girls, but, of course, they're gone, and Sammy's gesture of sympathy goes unnoticed. Again, even though Sammy acts not from the culture of place, but against it, we see the organic unity of setting, character, and plot.

## Landscape as conductor and container

One of my MFA students, Kyle Minor, has a wonderful essay, 'Lay Me Down in the Blue Grass,' which recently won second place in the student writing contest sponsored by *The Atlantic Monthly*. In the essay, he tells the story of his wife's nephew who committed suicide.

Set in Kentucky, the essay describes the day of the funeral and the burial. 'Imagine a Kentucky mountain as a landscape turned to anger,' Kyle writes, 'and needing to purge by the rushing of waters.'[11] Notice how the landscape takes on the emotions of the moment, yet another use for place in narrative, as a container for the emotions that are too complex and intense for the characters to hold inside. Eudora Welty, in her essay on place, talks about how the landscape of the setting creates the emotional life that is lived there, contributes to the authenticity and definition of characters, and allows what the writer has come to the page to say. For Welty, the setting of a piece of fiction is 'the ground conductor of all the currents of emotion and belief and moral conviction that charge out from the story in its course' (53–54).

As I've already suggested, I like to think of landscape as both conductor and receiver. A famous example is the end of James Joyce's story, 'The Dead,' where Gabriel listens to his wife's story of the frail, ill Michael Fury, a boy who loved her so deeply he left his sick bed and went out into the rainy night in hopes that he might persuade her to come downstairs from her grandmother's house and be with him one more time before she went away in the morning to the convent. Gretta sobs with the sad remembrance of how she told Michael to go home lest he 'get his death in the rain,' and how he told her 'he did not want to live.'[12] Gabriel must confront the truth of Michael Furey's great love for Gretta and the romance she once felt: 'He[Gabriel] had never felt like that himself towards any woman but he knew that such a feeling must be love' (725). Gabriel's own feeling of self-importance shrivels at the end of the story, and, in addition to his knowledge of the romance between Gretta and Michael, he also accepts the mortality that is the truth of all their lives: 'One by one they were all becoming shades' (725). The very last move of the story features the landscape, and Joyce's description illustrates how that landscape holds the emotions that Gabriel cannot express to Gretta. From their bedroom window, he watches the snow falling outside:

> Yes, the newspapers were right: snow was general all over Ireland. It was falling on every part of the dark, central plain, on the treeless hills, falling softly upon the Bog of Allen and, father westward, softly falling into the dark mutinous Shannon waves. It was falling, too, upon every part of the lonely churchyard on the hill where Michael Furey lay buried. It lay thickly drifted on the crooked crosses and headstones, on the spears of the little gate, on the barren thorns. His soul swooned slowly as he heard the snow falling faintly through the universe and faintly falling, like the descent of their last end, upon all the living and the dead. (725)

The smallness that Gabriel now feels, the diminished self-importance, is now projected out onto the landscape, particularly the churchyard where Michael Furey is buried, where everything is being covered with snow.

The uniqueness of place is endangered today; at least it's true in my part of the world. Builders build houses according to a handful of models. Franchise restaurants and shops replace independently owned businesses. Don't even get me started on how the discount store, *Wal-Mart*, has dried up the downtown business districts of thousands of small American cities. The truth is the landscape is becoming more and more homogenous and predictable these days. Thank god for the artists, then, who remind us of the particulars of our world. The fiction writer, for one, documents the individual, an act that can't take place without an intimate knowledge of the places that people occupy. Today, more than ever, it's important that writers understand how to evoke the unique qualities of landscapes by finding the details that distinguish them and then using those details to create characters, plots, and atmospheres. If you know your places fully – if your powers of observation are keen – you'll not only do a bang-up job of painting a picture of the setting, you'll also understand how landscape becomes necessary to the characters, their stories, their emotions, and to everything you've come to the page to express.

### Exercises

1. Choose a place that you know intimately. Start with a broad lens by choosing a city or a region, and then come up with as many concrete details as you can to describe the landscape. Pay attention to sensory details, not limiting yourself to the visual. What are the sounds of this place? The smells? The textures? The tastes? Then narrow your lens to a particular location on that landscape. A neighborhood, perhaps, or a particular street, or a certain part of the countryside. Again, find the sensory details that you might use to describe that landscape. Write a bit of description that contains at least one authenticating detail such as the sunlight on the tree trunks in Jewett's 'The White Heron,' or the plowed earth shining like metal in Steinbeck's 'The Chrysanthemums.'

2. Think about the customs and cultural attitudes of the people who populate the landscape you've described in exercise 1. How are the people similar to that landscape? What do they

do or say that connects them with the place where they live? Create a specific character and have that character engage in an activity that is common to his or her landscape – playing music for tips in the subway, for example, or planting flowers in the garden, or shearing sheep on a farm. Let that character's actions either be in harmony with the culture of the landscape or in resistance to that culture. If the former, experiment with how a visitor to that landscape can cause the character to question his or her place there. If the latter, see how the actions of another character, one more in harmony with the setting, can provide a means of dramatizing the tension between person and place.

3. Someone has just suffered a great loss or come to a startling knowledge in a public place where he or she doesn't want to show emotion. Using vivid, concrete details, describe the person and the surroundings. This is an exercise in letting the details of place contain the emotions that characters find difficult to express in words.

## Notes

1. J. Mellencamp, 'Small Town,' *Scarecrow*. Polygram Records. 1985.
2. E. Welty, *On Writing* (New York: Modern Library Edition/Random House, 2002), pp. 41–2.
3. P. Roth, 'The Conversion of the Jews,' *The Norton Anthology of Short Fiction*, 2nd edn, ed. R. V. Cassill (New York: W. W. Norton, 1981), pp. 1261–74.
4. W. Faulkner, Nobel Prize Speech. 10 December 1950. Rpt. on *William Faulkner on the Web*. 11 April 2005; 23 July 2005.
5. S. O. Jewett, 'A White Heron,' *The Story and Its Writer*, 4th edn, ed. A. Charters (Boston: Bedford Books of St. Martin's Press, 1995), p. 675. Cited hereafter as *The Story and Its Writer* with page number.
6. J. Conrad, Preface to *The Nigger of the Narcissus* (New York: The Heritage Press, 1965), p. xvii.
7. J. Gardner, *The Art of Fiction* (New York: Vintage, 1983), pp. 31–32.
8. J. Steinbeck, 'The Chrysanthemums,' *The Story and Its Writer*: 1206.
9. S. Dobyns, 'Kansas,' *The Best American Short Stories*, ed. A. Tan, series ed. K. Kenison (Boston: Houghton-Mifflin, 1999), pp. 48–49.
10. J. Updike, 'A & P,' *The Story and Its Writer*: 1280–84.
11. K. Minor, 'Lay Me Down in the Blue Grass,' Unpublished Essay, 2005.
12. J. Joyce, 'The Dead,' *The Story and Its Writer*: 724.

# Further Reading

L. Anderson (ed.), *Creative Writing: A Workbook with Readings* (London: Routledge/The Open University, 2006).

M. Arana (ed.), *The Writing Life* (New York: Public Affairs, 2003).

W. H. Auden, *The Dyer's Hand and Other Essays* (London: Faber and Faber, 2003).

P. Auster, *The Red Notebook* (London: Faber and Faber, 2005).

J. Bell (ed.), *The Creative Writing Course Book: Forty Authors Share Advice and Exercises for Fiction and Poetry* (London: Pan, 2001).

J. Bell and P. Magrs (eds.), *Pretext: Salvage* (Cambridge: University of East Anglia, 1999).

——, *Pretext Volume 2* (London: Pen & Inc., 2000).

A. Boulter, *Writing Fiction: Creative and Critical Approaches* (Basingstoke: Palgrave, 2006).

C. Boylan, *The Agony and the Ego: Art and Strategy of Fiction Writing Explored* (London: Penguin, 1993).

J. Campbell, *The Hero's Journey* (San Francisco: Harper, 1991).

J. Casterton, *Creative Writing: A Practical Guide* (Basingstoke: Palgrave, 2005).

A. Charters, *The Story and Its Writer* (Boston: Bedford Books of St Martin's Press, 1995).

P. Cobley, *Narrative* (London: Routledge, 2001).

P. Dunker (ed.), *Writing on the Wall: Selected Essays* (London: Rivers Oram, 2002).

M. Ellmann, *The Hunger Artists: Starving, Writing and Imprisonment* (Cambridge, Massachusetts: Havard, 1993).

E. M. Forster, *Aspects of the Novel* (Harmondsworth: Penguin, 1976).

P. Fussell, *Poetic Meter and Poetic Form* (New York: Random House, 1965).

J. Gardner, *The Art of Fiction* (New York: Vintage, 1983).

G. Harper (ed.), *Teaching Creative Writing* (New York: Continuum, 2006).

——, *The Creative Writing Guidebook* (New York: Continuum, 2007).

J. Hodgins, *A Passion for Narrative: A Guide for Writing Fiction* (New York: St Martin's Press, 1994 [1993]).

H. James, *Partial Portraits* (London: Macmillan, 1988).

R. Kee, *Story* (London: Methuen, 1999).

S. King, *On Writing: A Memoir of the Craft* (London: Hodder and Stoughton, 2000).

L. Lubbock, *The Craft of Fiction* (New York: Viking, 1957).

V. Nabokov, *Lectures on Literature*, ed. F. Bowers (New York: Harcourt Brace Jovanovich, 1980).

J. Newman, Edmund Cusick and Aileen La Tourette (eds.), *The Writer's Workbook* (London: Arnold, 2000).

C. Norman (ed.), *Poets on Poetry* (London: Collier-Macmillan, 1962).

P. Picasso, *Picasso on Art: A Selection of Views*, ed. D. Ashton (New York: Da Capo Press, 1972).

E. Welty, *One Writer's Beginnings* (Cambridge: Harvard University Press, 1984).

———, *On Writing* (New York: Modern Library Edition/Random House, 2002).

# Index